An Alternative Framework
for
Community Learning Centers
in the 21st Century:

A Systemic Design Approach
Toward the Creation of a
Transformational Learning System

by
Michael Frederick Reber

A Dissertation Presented To The Faculty
Of The Asia-Pacific Centers
Of The International University
In Partial Fulfillment Of The Requirements For
The Degree of Doctor of Philosophy
Education and Institutional Transformation

2002

An Alternative Framework for Community Learning Centers in the 21st Century:
A Systemic Design Approach Toward the Creation of a Transformational Learning System

Dissertation.com
USA • 2003

ISBN: 1-58112-182-2
www.Dissertation.com/library/1121822a.htm

This dissertation for the Doctor of Philosophy

degree by

Michael F. Reber

has been approved for the

Asia-Pacific Centers

by

Dayle M. Bethel

Dayle M. Bethel, Dissertation Advisor

Dean of The International University

Asia-Pacific Centers

Robert L. Fried

Robert L. Fried, Dissertation Member

Associate Professor of Northeastern University

School of Education

Rick Smyre

Rick Smyre, Dissertation Member

Doctoral Student Mentor of The International University

President of Communities Of The Future (COTF)

Date _January 27, 2003_

TABLE OF CONTENTS

Abstract

Public Community Learning Centers (CLCs), at least in the context of the United States, are social structures that have been established to address particular community needs. In the beginning, they were instituted as extensions of state departments' human services in order to assist communities with programs such as adult literacy and high school graduation certification. Today, they have taken on a broader role as a result of the Elementary and Secondary Education Act (Title X, Part I) that gives rural and inner-city public schools nearly $2 billion over five years (1999~2004) to develop CLCs for programs such as mentoring in basic skills or helping high school students prepare for college.

Despite these noble efforts, public CLCs are still not integral parts of community sustainability. One could argue that a major cause for this is that they are established mainly for political purposes. However, the problem is much deeper. Public CLCs today are unable to serve as sustainable social structures because they lack several foundational principles that assist communities with creating and maintaining sustainability. In short, they do not adequately reflect the values, beliefs, and knowledge of the current community education movement. Thus, an alternative framework within which communities can develop CLCs is needed.

Using a systemic design approach toward the design of a community learning system, an alternative framework for CLCs is designed that enables communities to create the conditions whereby they can become self-reliant, self-governing, and sustainable.

Introduction

The community learning network is a framework proposed by scholars such as Ivan Illich, Malcolm Knowles, Bela Banathy, James Moffett, and Charles Reigeluth that enables communities to create the conditions for self-reliance, self-governance, and sustainability. Each of these scholars has created an approach for developing and implementing a community learning network. Bela Banathy's "Design Architecture" is one approach that has been helpful for communities and which is the method employed in this treatise.

Systemic Design Architecture is a design approach toward all social systems and consists of five iterative cycles: initial exploration, knowledge base, description of outcomes, evaluation and experimentation, and design solution. It is appropriate for designing a community learning network because it can assist a community with revisiting and refining its values and beliefs and incorporating principles of *participatory democratic action.* This in turn creates the necessary conditions whereby a community can, increasingly, become more self-reliant, self-governing, and sustainable. In addition, all members of the community, not just those elected to the school board or parents of children who attend public schools, participate in the design solution of the learning system. This activity includes defining what the system is and what the system will do for learners, addressing the specifications, describing the system's functions, and finally, defining the enabling systems which typically are the management system, the organization, and the systemic environment of the learning network.

Using Systemic Design Architecture to design an alternative framework for community learning centers in this treatise, several conclusions can be drawn.

The kind of society that the learning system should help to create is one in which every individual discovers his innate potential and lives a life that is commensurate with his self and others in order to, through participatory democratic actions, create a culture that develops and sustains the political, cultural, economic, and environmental spheres of society.

This vision of society is complemented by a vision of a future learning system. The learning system should be an open and transformational learning environment that exists to assist individuals with discovering and actualizing their innate potentials; transmitting to them cultural roles; conveying to them values of the culture; assisting them in learning how to search for truth, beauty, and good, and to create value in the world; developing in them competency in the culture's notational systems; providing them guidance, coaching, teaching, and training in the human domains of society; and encouraging experts in their respective fields to participate in the educational endeavor of the learning system.

The visions are actualized within the context of current realities. Some of the realities include cognitive and human growth, sociocultural, economic, socio-technological, technological, scientific, and organizational realities. Some of the implications of these realities entail a more learner-centered educational environment and a transformation *in the relationship* between the four spheres of society.

Some of the values to which the members of the new learning system adhere include recognizing the dignity and uniqueness of each individual and organizing learning around the cognitive abilities of each person in order to assist him with actualizing his inherent potential.

Using the visions and realities as a knowledge base, an image of the future learning system is created. Some of the elements of the image include the contention that education SHOULD assist an individual with actualizing his potential and that education SHOULD be organized around the cognitive abilities of each person.

The core ideas that help shape the learning system include the principles of self-actualization, brain-based learning and theory of multiple intelligences, symbolic interactionist social psychology, self-government, learner-centered and learner-directed education, and systemic design.

In order to implement the image, a mission statement and purposes are developed. One mission of the learning system is to maximize the greatest benefits for individuals in their development toward self-actualization. In addition to the mission statement, the statement of purposes explains the arrangements and relationships within the community learning network, such as creating a society in which all four social spheres are arranged and integrated in such a way as to assist individuals with actualizing their true potentials.

The mission and purposes of the new learning system transform the definition of community learning centers into one that acknowledges a holistic outlook toward life and learning. Some of the new aspects of CLCs include: 1) becoming a "node" in the learning network that helps to facilitate learning and network relationships in order to maximize the total benefits of the system, 2) providing for learners of all ages learning resources and arrangements that assist them in actualizing their true potentials, and 3) encouraging the creation of a true learning society in which all individuals are able to contribute to one another's learning despite geographical differences.

In summary, systemic design architecture transforms the narrow utilitarian definition of community learning centers into a holistic and life-actualizing definition that is inclusive of the entire community. CLCs within the framework of a community learning network are located in different places throughout the community, such as school buildings, local business offices, or people's homes. Furthermore, within this framework CLCs fill a multitude of communal learning functions that assist in the natural process of community sustainability and self-reliance.

The picture that I have briefly presented is based upon some basic assumptions that must be clarified before proceeding with a comprehensive discussion on the topic of public community learning networks. First, what I mean by *public* is that which affects or concerns the community or the people. Second, *community* is differentiated from "society-at-large." As David Norton states, society-at-large is about impersonal association (1991, 146):

> Relations among persons who appear to one another not as persons, that is, unified totalities that are ends in themselves, but rather as compartmented roles, offices, skills, and so forth. Relations in society-at-large are impersonal because they are utility relations, others appearing to each in but the aspect according to the needs of each, and not for what they are in themselves.

Community, on the other hand, as Walter Nicgorski describes, "is rooted in the individual and is formed, led and enriched by distinct responsible persons. Rather than a collectivity of people, it is a mutual sharing of their particular endowments" (1986, 326). It is, overall, about interpersonal association, the "form of association intermediate between the individual and society-at-large" (Norton 1991, 138). It is comprised of integrated persons who interact with one another as "whole persons" (ibid.):

> Everything that is the person is continuous with what appears in each expression and supportive of it....Each of a person's expressions reflect one or another of her life-shaping choices and her life-shaping choices are themselves complementary to one another and contributory in their distinctive ways to the individual's enterprise of self-actualization.

Furthermore, these integrated persons find solidarity in certain shared beliefs that are "embodied in institutions and practices," and it is within this context that people come to acknowledge those who are members and non-members of the community and to care for one another as whole persons (ibid.). This caring is best actualized when conditions exist to assist people with doing self-fulfilling work.

With this understanding of community, *education* is defined as the drawing out of one's inherent potential in accordance with the principles that govern each stage of life. Childhood is a stage for exploring one's immediate world, beginning with the family and moving outward into the community. As the child explores his world and engages in meaningful activity that is commensurate with his interests, abilities, and inclinations, he acquires necessary skills at an elementary level that imitate those skills for the performance of social roles in later life. Adolescence is a time for self-discovery, the answering of the question, "Who am I?" which requires society to provide young people opportunities to experience alternative social roles or lives and to recognize mistakes as part of the educational process of discovering one's true self. Maturity is a time for actualizing the life that one has chosen to live. The mature individual is self-governing and requires opportunities to further the development of his growth, in a term, "self-fulfilling work." Society must provide the conditions that enable people to do the work that is theirs to do in life. Finally, old age is a time for reflection and the contribution of experience and wisdom to the next generation. Senior citizens should be regarded as important educational resources for all the preceding stages of life.

Public Education for an American Republic is education that is available to all members of a community. It is the *complementarity and congeniality* of private and civil association within the public sphere for the purposes of assisting persons with identifying and drawing out their inherent potentials and helping them to actualize those potentials. The implication of this idea is that the responsibility for education lies solely in the hands of the members of the community and not government. Hence, to entrust government to be the primary benefactor, standard setter, and overseer of public education only leads to political and educational lethargy on the part of the populace; thus eroding democratic, republican self-government.

Government has two roles in a healthy society. At one level it must be a "monopoly of coercive power" that provides for public safety, law enforcement, and national defense (Norton 1991, 170). For Americans, it must protect our Bill of Rights and those rights expressed in the state constitutions. On another level it must be a conducive power that "affords to the persons who comprise its constituency the requisite social conditions for leading the best lives possible," i.e. subsistence and enablement (ibid., ix). This is in alignment with John Dewey's two criteria for a democratic society as stated in, *Democracy and Education*: (1) providing a numerous and varied amount of interests that are consciously shared amongst members of the community and which are relied upon in guiding society, and (2) maintaining a fuller and freer interplay of the various forms of private and civil association that the members can enjoy which in turn affect social habits in the democratic community (1997, 86-87). Thus, the development, financing, and implementation of a public community learning network occurs via the private and civil associations of the community with government providing a "conducive" environment to let them do so.

Because individuals are complementing each other's personal excellences within a context of congenial relationships, people who do not necessarily share common values, interests and ideals can create a public community learning network. Randy Hewitt purports that "the democratic ideal refers to the faith in the individual to define and develop her particular capacities in harmony with the needs and demands of others as they define and develop their own powers" (2002, 8).   Hewitt continues, "As a standard of judgment, the ideal refers to the degree to which happiness and harmony are brought about in actual effect of acting upon her idea of the good.   It follows, then, that the individual has the right and duty to act with common good in mind.   And, as new potentials are realized, new consequences, demands, and claims of right emerge that require a recalibration of action and a broader idea of a common good" (ibid.).

A person acting within the context that Hewitt describes is the embodiment of those values and beliefs that Norton refers to as, *noblesse oblige*, "persons recognize that their responsibility for continuous moral growth is their responsibility for progressively more elevated moral conduct" (1991, xii).   This is not an elitist or utopian ideal.   It is an ideal that every person strives to achieve at his particular stage of life.   Therefore, a child cannot be held accountable to the demands of an adolescent and an adolescent cannot be held accountable to the demands of an adult.   Each has its own place and its own principles for character development that a person is responsible for achieving.

Character development is categorically entwined with equity.   According to Hewitt (2002, 9):

> That the democratic problem is a practical one suggests that it gets its concrete form and meaning from within the various associations that individuals share with each other. Therefore, the particular meaning of liberty, equality, justice, and hence power are determined

by individuals as they define and measure the particular consequences of acting for some specific good upon the growth of their individual capacities and upon the shared conditions that nourish this growth....Democracy in general can be realized only to the degree that the individuals put it into practice through the particular shared activities that define them and give them purpose. A more just and enriching relation between the development of one's potential and that of all others can be established, refined, and expanded only to the extent that individuals strive to be thoughtful, appreciative, and understanding of each other in everything they do.

Equity can be further explained in terms of proportional equality. As Plato quotes Socrates in *The Republic*, "We are not born all exactly alike but different in nature, for all sorts of different jobs" (*Book II*, 168). This can be differentiated into *proportional productive equality* and *proportional recipient equality*. Proportional productive equality "obtains when A and B are alike doing the work for which each is by nature best suited" (Norton 1991, 161). This holds that government has a responsibility to create the conditions that provide people ample opportunities to do the self-fulfilling work that is theirs to do, and the nature of each community will determine the management of its members into the *right* work. Right work in this context is work that exists or has the potential to exist in the community that can be done by those people who have the commensurable nature and capacities to do the work. This extends beyond the limits of racial, physical, cultural, or gender equity. Funding and access are available to all in accordance with each person's nature and capacities and the management structure of the system.

Proportional recipient equality "obtains when A and B alike possess the particular goods and utilities to which each is entitled" (ibid.). This means that not all people will be entitled to all goods, but all people will be entitled to only those goods that assist with their self-actualization. And who determines this? For Plato in *The Republic* he believed that it is was the role of the Guardians. But for an American Republic, the responsibility rests in the hands of mature, self-governing individuals. For children and adolescents, the process of entitlement is assisted by parents, the extended family, teachers, mentors, guides, and coaches. It does not rest in the hands of our current guardians, i.e. the school board, state boards of education, the federal government, or presidential blue-ribbon committees. Each person is entitled to those goods that he requires for his self-development and the limits of one's entitlement is determined by the course one chooses in his life. Norton expresses this in the following manner (1991, 121-122):

> The individual who possesses self-knowledge and lives by it manifests justice, first by not laying claim to goods that he or she cannot utilize, and second by actively willingly such goods into the hands of those who can utilize them toward self-actualization. What is expressed in both cases is not "selflessness," but the proportionality of a self-responsible self that is situated in relations of interdependence with other selves that are, or ought to be, self-responsible. An individual who possesses self-knowledge and lives by its direction recognizes goods to which he or she is not entitled as distractions from his or her proper course of life...And to will to others their true utilities is at the same time the concrete expression of respect for them as ends in themselves and recognition that we stand to gain from the worthy living of others.

In conclusion, the learning system proposed in the following pages recognizes the dignity of the human being and his integral relationship with community. It is by re-organizing learning systems around individuals that a clearer understanding of community is realized. Thus, a public community learning network is not created by atomized individuals who have conflicting values and beliefs and who view themselves as utilities, but "whole" people who see themselves on journeys of self-development that ends only at death. In order to guide people on their journeys in a most equitable and humane way, tools are provided, such as the voucher system (it is more of a pass than a voucher), which are developed by the community via private and civil associations in cooperation with local government. Though all communities are different and have varying notions of "community," the learning system should never undermine a people's right to equal access and opportunities to those goods and utilities that are required at the appropriate times of their learning and self-actualization.

Part 1
Review of Literature

Introduction

Part 1 is a review of the literature on community learning and Community Learning Centers (CLCs). The term "community learning" or "learning-in-community" is employed instead of "community education" in order to distinguish between the two meanings. Within the "community-and-learning/education" movement, two distinct concepts regarding the relationship of learning and community have developed. According to Robert Fried, *learning-in-community* emphasizes "community-based *learning* processes," whereas *community education* focuses on "the delivery of educational *programs*."

Chapter 1, "CLCs—Past and Present," reviews various case studies of CLCs in both the public and private sectors. It begins with a summary of the earliest documented public CLC, the New York City CUE CLC Program, and continues with an analysis of two other public CLCs. Following discussion of the public CLCs is a look at one example of a fully integrated CLC system, the Jewish Community Centers of Chicago with a history dating back to 1903.

Chapter 2, "Community Learning Concept Contributors," reviews some key scholars who have developed the idea of community learning networks and community learning centers. Specifically, the work of Ivan Illich, Malcolm Knowles, Bela Banathy, James Moffett, Charles M. Reigeluth, and Robert L. Fried is explored. Illich's concept of the learning "web" is recognized. In addition, Knowles' conceptual framework within which all social systems are viewed as systems of learning resources is discussed. Banathy's "Learning Society" is referred to as well as his method of systemic design of learning systems.   The educational contributions of Moffett are acknowledged, especially his vision of "the universal schoolhouse" and its emphasis on systemic problem solving, open system of education, and moral democratic society. Also considered is Reigeluth, a systemic design colleague of Banathy, who perceives the CLC as a component within a transformational learning system.   Finally, Fried's contribution to the concept of the CLC during his work with eight communities in New Hampshire from 1973 through 1975 on the CLC Project is presented.

Chapter 1: CLCs—Past and Present (1969 through Today)

This paper focuses on a few CLCs even though an abundance of models could be addressed. The intention is to shed light on the different learning systems in which CLCs are grounded. The CLCs that are addressed include the New York City CUE CLC, USAID LearnLink, the federally funded 21st Century CLC Program, and the Jewish Community Centers of Chicago.

New York City CUE CLC Program

Background

The New York City Center for Urban Education (CUE) established its first Community Learning Center (CLC) Program in 1969 for the South Bronx and the Williamsburg area of Brooklyn. The program's mission was to create better communication between schools, parents, and the greater community (1971a, 1-5). As CUE recognizes in, *Ways of Establishing and Funding CLCs* (1971a, 1),

> From one city to the next, community mistrust of what goes on in the buildings called schools emerges as a persistent and pervasive deterrent to establishing the level of communication necessary for effective education. Equally many school people often regard with suspicion any parents or other community residents who express close interest in their educational activities. Thus, despite the polite rhetoric which is designed to mask the extent of the severely strained relationship between school and urban community, more and more the widespread disillusionment with traditional public education unabashedly occupies the attention of community groups. The schools are perceived as irrelevant to the needs and interests of the urban community and, with few exceptions, they are.

Assumptions

   Three assumptions served as the basis for the conception of the CLC that the New York City CUE developed. These included an expansion of urbanization, increase in society's technological needs, and continuance of participatory democracy in both action and belief (ibid., 2). Furthermore, these three assumptions had at least three implications. The first implication was a need for an enlightened electorate who was capable of meeting requirements such as technological literacy, political participation, and virtuous living. The second implication was the creation of an educational system that could communicate and interact with its clients responsibly. The final implication was the creation of self-governing communities that were capable of understanding their own needs and wants and in turn creating an educational system that was able to produce future generations that were capable of doing the same within a pluralistic social framework (ibid.).

CUE's Definition of a CLC

   The purpose of the CUE CLC Program was to enhance communication between the schools, parents, and greater community. CUE defined CLCs as (ibid., 3),

> Settings in which educational activities and meetings take place. They are strategically located within the community. As envisioned, the Centers should exist independently of the school system, and therefore be funded by other sources such as foundations, the federal government, private organizations, and universities...The community learning center [should] be a place which fosters easy exchange of ideas, and a productive working together of school personnel and community persons.

Other attributes of a CUE CLC included staff, personnel, and costs.   The staff developed and evaluated programs and designed research.   It was also knowledgeable about the community for which it was serving, such as the kinds of programs that were already serving the community, school and community demographics, school data, school enrollment figures, and information regarding parent participation in the school (ibid., 5).   Furthermore, the staff included members of the community and adequately reflected its culture and beliefs.   For example, if a CLC were situated in a predominately Spanish-speaking community, then the staff of that CLC was bilingual and lived in the community.

The personnel were both paid personnel and volunteers from within the community.   Volunteers were part-time high school students, college students studying to be teachers or social workers, or full-time retirees.   They assisted in a variety of ways.   Full-time retirees were valuable because they had experiences that they could share, such as assisting with office management or program development (ibid., 7).

A final key attribute of a CUE CLC was its costs.   The budget for a CLC was supported by outside sources, such as the state or federal government or foundations.   Costs included fixed and variable costs, such as salaries, office supplies, and electricity (ibid., 9).

In addition to the aforementioned attributes of CLCs, CUE distinguished between CLCs and Community Centers.   Though community centers had some of the attributes of CLCs, they did not have them all.   CLCs were considered to be legitimate organizations in the view of the community, the political establishments, and the educational practitioners.   The programs, projects, and curricula of CLCs were integrated into the school curricula.   In addition, the programs offered by the CLCs were both formal and informal.   Another attribute of the CLCs was their location.   All of the CLCs were located in an area that was accessible to both community members and school officials (1971a, 4).

Mission and Goals of a CUE CLC

The mission of a CUE CLC was "to improve the quality of the transactions between school systems and the publics they serve" (1971e, 1).   This mission was supported by three goals.   The first was to provide a neutral environment in which both school officials and community members were able to discuss educational problems. The second was to serve as a resource center for both school officials and community members regarding educational issues.   The final goal was to serve as a mechanism for translating community educational needs into developmental projects (ibid.).

The CUE CLC Program Components

The first CUE CLC that was established served "as a resource center for community residents on educational issues" and as "a mechanism for increasing program interface" (1971e, 2-3).   The components of the CUE CLC Program included three sub-programs: The Educational Leadership Development Program (ELDP), The Parent Participation Workshop Program (PPWP), and The School-Community Relations Program (SCRP) (ibid.)[1].

---

[1]For purposes of this paper, only the ELDP is reviewed because of its significant impact upon the lives of those

These sub-programs were mutually exclusive in the first year that they were implemented—"no formal attempt was made to interrelate the programs, and no sessions or special events were arranged to bring participants in the various programs or subgroups in contact with each other" (ibid.).   However, in the following years, CUE worked to establish stronger communications between the three sub-programs via field administrators.   The field administrators were responsible for three key aspects of communication between the sub-programs.   The first was to act as liaison between the CLC and the central CUE office regarding administrative matters.   The second was to create a communications network between community-based educational interest groups, community leaders, and school personnel.   The third was to allocate and utilize space in the CLC for functions not directly related to the programs (ibid., 2-3).

Educational Leadership Developmental Program (ELD Program)

Participants in the ELD Program

The program took place at the South Bronx CLCs and the Williamsburg area of Brooklyn and included two hundred trainees that participated in the program from fall of 1970 to spring of 1971.   The predominant groups were Puerto Ricans and African-Americans.   One of the objectives of the CUE staff was to increase the level of cooperative interaction between these two groups (1971f, 8-9).

Goal

The most important goal of the ELD Program was "increasing a sense of community, unifying community residents to present a united front in presenting

---

involved in the program, the schools, and the greater community to which all belonged.

problems to school personnel, and increasing the influence of community forces in school decision-making" (1971f, 7).

<u>Short-Term Objectives</u>

The short-term objectives of the ELD Program were to develop a group of individuals who could understand the systemic relationships within the educational system, discover the important roles they could play within the educational system so as to improve the quality of the community's educational programs, and help improve the communication between the school and the community (1971b, 1).

<u>Long-Term Objectives</u>

The long-term objectives of the ELD Program fell into three categories or programs: A) Leadership Development, B) Community Intervention, and C) Research & Development.

A) Leadership Development

The objectives for Leadership Development that were set by CUE included the following: 1) to provide information to program participants about the structure and functioning of the local school system as well as those institutions and agencies that related in some way to the school system, 2) to assist program participants in developing those necessary skills for solving educational problems, 3) to develop within the program participants a disposition toward action and organization as a way to deal with community-school problems, and 4) to develop the program participants into capable community leaders (1971b, 1).

In order to develop the leadership qualities necessary for the trainees, the curriculum focused on educational problems that the local community and African-American and Puerto Rican students faced. In addition, it focused on the structure of the school system, such as the decentralization of the system, how the system interacts with various agencies, the school curriculum, and special education programs. Finally, it considered the roles of parents, their rights, the Parent Association, and how they could be more active in the system (1971f, 4-5).

The skills the Leadership Development Program focused on were identifying problems, determining which information is necessary to solve the problems, and organizing other people in order to make the best of human resources in solving the problems (ibid., 5). Specifically, trainees learned how to discuss problems with school personnel and officials, lead in group discussions, role play in order to better understand opposing views on issues, interview people in order to become skilled at gathering data, use various kinds of information in order to evaluate schools and school systems, and organize people into groups in order to solve a problem (ibid.).

Action orientation was another area that the program concentrated on for developing qualified community leaders in education. The orientations that the trainees became accustomed to involved a willingness to become active in solving a problem, a belief that one is able to accomplish a task through action, a belief that school officials are capable of being more responsive to complaints or protests, and a desire to make the community a more integrated part of the decision-making processes within the school (ibid.).

The "critical criterion" that determined the success of the Leadership Development Program was leadership behavior. It was measured according to various indicators: attending meetings, serving as officers, organizing and leading a group, acting as a resource person, training others in the group, acting as a liaison between the community and the school, gaining employment with schools or other community organizations, and working to change policy for the betterment of the school, students, and the greater community (ibid., 5-6).

B) Community Intervention

The objectives of the Community Intervention aspect of the ELD Program included the development of community leaders who would in turn develop others to be actively involved in community-school issues, increase community participation in school issues, and develop cooperative working relations between the community members of different ethnic origins in order to better influence the effectiveness of community in community-school decision-making processes (1971b, 1).

The hoped for outcome of the Community Intervention aspect of the ELD Program was a multiplier effect. A small group of citizens were trained as community leaders in education and they in turn encouraged others to participate in educational matters. The model that CUE developed for "community impact" is illustrated in Figure 1.

Figure 1. Community Impact Model (1971f, 7)

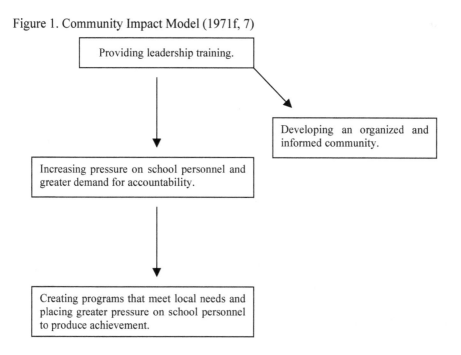

C) Research and Development Effort

The first immediate objective for the Research and Development Effort included the construction of a development model of community educational leadership development that could be replicated and introduced in other communities. The second was the contribution to a better understanding of community development and the roles that research and development agencies may play in such an effort (1971b, 1-2).

Strategies for the ELD Program

The strategies that were employed to implement ELD included two cycles of the program with each cycle running for fifteen weeks, two four hour class sessions, one three hour field work session, and a curriculum that included four units (1971b, 2):

1. Local Educational Leadership and Problems—addressed leadership and the impact ethnic group history and culture have on educational issues.

2. The School—addressed the organization, school jargon, curriculum, accountability, and evaluation of the schools.

3. School and Community Relations—addressed the relationship that the school has with the community.

4. Public Education—addressed all aspects of the public educational system.

Also noted in the report regarding the ELD Program was the significance of the field manual. It not only provided the curriculum for the program, but also served as important reference material for program developers to use in other urban areas (ibid., 4-5).

Findings of ELD Program

The ELD Program was first conceived by the CUE staff as a training program; however, over time the program began to focus on community impact and research and development (ibid., 9). The training program progressed the fastest, followed by community impact, and lastly by research and development (ibid.).

CUE contends that as a training program, the ELD Program was highly successful and had a great impact upon the participants' acquisition and development of factual information (ibid., 10). They showed "substantial gains" in skill development. The greatest gains were made in evaluating school effectiveness, leading group discussions, role playing, and organizing community people for action (ibid.). Also, the trainees were putting to use what they had learned in the fifteen week sessions. CUE reports that many of the participants had started attending school and community organizational meetings, holding executive positions in these organizations, training others to become more active in community organizations, and often speaking to audiences with greater confidence and skill (ibid., 18). Furthermore, one-fifth of those who participated in the CUE program found jobs in schools or community organizations (ibid.).

Conclusion

The CUE CLC Program demonstrates that becoming an active member in the educational endeavor of one's community is an important aspect of learning-in-community. By empowering themselves with the skills to ask questions and identify problem-situations, ascertain which information will assist in making the most appropriate decisions, and discuss those ideas with other community members, parents are able to contribute more effectively to the endeavor of participatory democratic action in education.

USAID LearnLink Project

Background

      LearnLink was established in 1996 by the U.S. Agency for International Development (USAID) Global Bureau under contract for the implementation of USAID's Global Communications and Learning Activity. The LearnLink activities are implemented in cooperation with the Academy for Educational Development (AED) at USAID (LearnLink 2000, "details", 1).

      The primary mission of LearnLink is to strengthen learning systems for sustainable development through the application of information, communication and educational technologies (IECTs); to improve people's ability to access educational resources using IECTs that link people and organizations; to accomplish those tasks identified by USAID Missions, Bureaus and offices for specific developing country contexts; and to create a replicable model for the application of educational technologies, such as the establishment of guidelines and strategies for assessment, implementation, institutionalization, sustainability, and monitoring and evaluation (ibid.).

Participant Nations

      LearnLink reports three nations as being participants in their community learning center program (LearnLink 2000, "task", 1). These nations include Benin, Ghana, and Paraguay. The CLC Program in Benin was designed in cooperation with the Africa Bureau Leland Initiative and with USAID/Cotonou. The purpose of the Benin Program was to "increase opportunities for learning in Africa through access to the Internet and to information, education and communications technologies" (ibid.).

14

The Ghana Program was created in cooperation with three Non-Government Organizations (NGOs) in order to "enhance basic education, train teachers, develop local businesses, strengthen municipal administration and civil society organizations, and provide health care information" (ibid.).   The Paraguay Program was done with The Municipality of Asunción.   The CLCs in this city are referred to as Amic@s (Aulas municipales de información, comunicación y aprendizaje).   The purpose of the program was to establish twelve CLCs in public buildings and municipal centers throughout the city in order to "provide basic education, communication, and information services to less advantaged citizens" (ibid.).   An important characteristic of the Amic@s is their emphasis on "the educational and civic development benefits of computers and communications in technology, specifically their ability to increase access to basic education resources, life-long learning opportunities, and information and services from municipal sources" (ibid.).

The Benin Program: Centre Songhaï

One of the most successful CLC projects that LearnLink participated in was the development of Centre Songhaï's Community Networking Service Centers (CNSCs). Centre Songhaï is an international NGO that conducts "research to improve the techniques of agricultural and animal cultivation by using local resources" (Centre Songhaï, "publication-english", 1).   It operates with the support of groups in Europe, America, Asia, and Africa.   LearnLink assisted Songhaï with activities such as establishing multi-media capable pilot CNSCs and providing training and technical assistance for both Center and Songhaï staff (Benin Country Paper 1999, 6).

15

The mission of Centre Songhaï is "to promote agricultural entrepreneurship among the young Africans while developing and transmitting appropriate human values for a change of behavior so that they become actors of their own development, capable of initiative and creativeness" (Centre Songhaï, "acceuil", 1).   It is guided by the vision of the Dominican priest, Father Nzamujo who is currently Director of the Center.

Father Nzamujo envisions Africa becoming sustainable through the development of production systems that create sustainable communities.   Instead of adopting the Western conception of development that emphasizes Gross National Product (GNP), he believes that development should be "grassroots," that is, development should explore ways in which the local environment can be used to create a sustainable community.   When speaking of Africa, he employs an African definition of development, which is the development of "production systems based on the relative or comparative advantage of Africa" (Benin Country Paper 1999, 2).   This means that those things that are distinctly African should serve as the basis of the African economic order, such as the heat, humidity, insects and plants, and African cultural heritage. Father Nzamjo believes that African people "must be capable of harnessing the resources around them" and using them in a sustainable manner (ibid.).

The way in which Father Nzamjo assists communities in Benin with actualizing this vision is through the use of technology centers.   Centre Songhaï serves as the hub for maintaining the important network between the communities in the outer fringes of Benin or the "outback" as the people of Benin refer to it.   In the "outback," CNSCs are created to transmit information.   Because of power constraints, solar power and high frequency microwave links and high frequency radio technology are used to ensure reliable, fast communication (ibid., 4).   With this electronic infrastructure, small villages can communicate with one another about their activities.   Through these technologies information is transmitted ubiquitously.   Father Nzamujo's description of a fish farm elucidates their work and its importance as a model for the development of sustainable communities (Benin Country Paper 1999, 8).

> We've beaten the University in growing Talapia (cat fish).   They got 1.4 gram per day, we get 1.6!   We produce 4 tons of insect larvae per month to feed the fish.   These insects never take a day off!   We raise 3,000 chicks per week, and from the chicken houses we take the droppings to feed the insects.   It keeps the insects away from us!

> One boy put small palm lamps onto the fish ponds.   It attracts the bugs, they get their wings wet and then the fish eat them!   The youth compete at creating new ways!

> Usually only 10% of catfish survive.   In the west [*sic*] *you* increase that by running water, which is a real waste.   These fish spawn during the rainy season.   We stimulate the rainy season with a shower head!   Then we lower the water level and remove the parents, so they won't eat the eggs.   30% of eggs hatch.   Usually the fish are killed by ammonia that is released when the other eggs decay.   So we add bacillus that attach to the old eggs and encapsulate the ammonia.   Then we add daphnia to eat the bacillus and free oxygen.   We get a 90% survival rate, and we've doubled the growth rate.

Conclusion

The application of CNSCs in Benin is one example of Alvin Toffler's "Third-Wave Effect." The "Third-Wave Effect" is when a very underdeveloped community employs advanced technologies that work to enhance the life of the community without jeopardizing its environmental, economic, or cultural sustainability. Thus, it is not necessary for a First-Wave (agricultural) society, such as a village in Benin, to become a Second-Wave (industrial) society in order to become a Third-Wave (information/technology) society. Many economists still argue, "We need to increase GNP of underdeveloped nations so they can be just like us!" In other words, they need to become industrialized countries before they can become technology countries. But the Songhaï model supports the argument that this is not necessary, and that development of CLCs within a sustainable framework like the one that Father Nzamujo employs is more likely to help communities help themselves.

U.S. 21ˢᵗ Century CLC Program

Background

On January 25th, 1994 the U.S. Congress passed into law *H.R. 6: Improving America's Schools Act* that extended for a five year period "the authorizations of appropriations for the programs under the Elementary and Secondary Education Act of 1965" (US Dept of Ed., "ESEA", 1). One of the programs included in the legislation was "Title X: Part I—21ˢᵗ Century Community Learning Centers" (ibid., 10). The title awarded $20,000,000 to public schools so they could be left open as CLCs during non-school hours (ibid., "sec. 1097", 1). It also made the following conclusions about schools: 1) they often serve as the best locations for providing education and human services to communities, 2) they often provide these services best when they cooperate with other agencies and organizations in the community, 3) they are often utilized more efficiently when provided for use to the entire community, 4) they are often the best locations for serving as centers for lifelong learning and educational opportunities, and 5) as 21ˢᵗ Century Community Learning Centers they are able to address many of the educational needs of the community (ibid., "sec. 10902", 1).

In order for a school to establish a CLC, Title X required the school to "plan, implement, or expand community learning centers" which included no less than four of the following programs and/or services. The kinds of educational programs include literacy, senior citizen, integrated education, health, social service, recreational, cultural, summer and weekend, nutrition and health, telecommunications and technology, and parenting skills programs. The kinds of services include children's day care, expanded library service hours, child day care providers support and training services, school drop-out services, disability services, and employment counseling, training, and placement services (ibid., "sec. 10905", 1).

The 21ˢᵗ Century CLC Program has received an extension of time in *Title 20— Education, Chapter 70—Strengthening and Improvement of Elementary and Secondary Schools, Subchapter X—programs of National Significance, Part I—21ˢᵗ Century Community Learning Centers* (US Code, "Title 20"). Similarly to "Improving America's Schools Act of 1994," *Title 20* continues to employ the same findings and regulations for public school CLC development.

Purposes of the 21ˢᵗ Century CLC Program

The purposes for having public schools as CLCs are best explained in the National Community Education Association and the U.S. Department of Education's 1997 report, *Keeping Schools Open As CLCs: Extending Learning in a Safe, Drug-Free Environment Before and After School.* The report states that public schools serve as the best venues for public CLCs. They provide a safe and drug-free environment for children to learn and grow. They cost less and are more accessible for extended learning. They have the resources to assist children with meeting the *America Reads Challenge* and with their other studies, such as algebra and geometry. They have the resources for mentoring in achieving basic skills as well as opportunities in finding an avocation that could become a lifelong interest. They can allow all participants in an educational system to come together to assist a child in meeting educational goals and objectives (ibid., ii).

Implicit Goals of the 21st Century CLC Program

Though not entirely explicit, public CLCs seem to be geared more toward extending *Goals 2000: Title III* than toward assisting communities to become sustainable entities via a transformational educational process. The report published by Designs for Learning, *Community Learning Centers: Design Specifications*, outlines key elements of a public CLC, two of which are standards and assessment. The report repeatedly emphasizes the importance of standards, normed reference testing, and outcome-based education. It specifically states the following about standards and assessment (1994, 3):

- Standards for student attainment must be world class—of a caliber that meets or exceeds the achievement of any student in the world. Standards are benchmarked at grades 4, 8, and 12 using state standards and emerging professional association standards for achievement and performance. Standards are of two types: performance outcomes and content mastery in five core subjects of math, science, English, geography, and history, plus the arts.

- Assessment of achievement is in part embedded into daily work and evaluated through competency expectations, exhibitions, portfolios, or presentations and checked against nationally normed tests. Community input is essential in establishing exacting standards.

- Curriculum is designed down from outcomes. Sites design powerful learning experiences that provide for development of skills, knowledge and attitudes and assist learners in achieving the standards and outcomes by choosing from a broad range of possibilities.

Students are also emphasized in the report (ibid., 5).

> Students are viewed as powerful resources, rather than as problems. When valued, students make an enormous contribution to the enterprise. They are an untapped resource and must become an integral part of staffing. Their active participation in decisions about the school and their own program contributes to their cognitive development and adds a considerable measure of deep connection. Their contributions of ideas and actions increases the pool of creative thinking for problem solving and their school service responsibilities lightens the work load for all.

Questionable Purposes

Though the 21ˢᵗ Century CLC Program seems to address the concerns of children and community, these purposes are questionable since they are juxtaposed with learner-centered educational principles and current research in human growth and development. Instead of being viewed as persons, children are viewed as workers who "make an enormous contribution to the enterprise." They are also viewed as "an untapped resource" that is to become an "integral part" of the enterprise. The report does not address students as human beings who have their own desires and unique ways of learning, but as a resource ready to be refined into a commodity.

Another criticism of the report is its attention toward parents' involvement in the educational process (ibid.).

> Parents need to have crucial roles in the learning of their children and the functioning of the school. Therefore, the program vigorously involves parents in their child's education in several ways: participating in student advisor conferences for goal setting; helping determine paths to goals; reviewing progress regularly; sharing skills and experiences; providing home-based learning reinforcement; and participating in governance.

Despite the report mentioning "decentralized decision making" and "parental involvement," these are contradicted by the lauding of standards and assessment. As James Moffett argues about *Goals 2000* in *The Universal Schoolhouse*, "You can't have it both ways—choice *and* standardization. Enforcing *conformity* as a way to *innovate* characterizes this centralized approach masquerading as grass roots experimentation: 'You are free to use any means to reach our goals as measured by our tests'" (1994, 125).

Moffett is not the only one to be critical of these purposes of education. Steve Parson, a former Mott Foundation Intern with the Western Michigan University Community Education Leadership Program and former President of the National Community Education Association, is just as condemning in *"Afterschool Programs: A Beginning, Not an End!"* He recognizes that the community education movement was in jeopardy because the public had placed too much pressure on accountability and standardized testing in the schools. This in turn diverted attention away from connecting community with the school and instead focused on the internal processes of producing high test scores (August 2000, 1). His greatest concern is that "we run the risk of sending the message that all it takes for a school to become a 'Community

Learning Center' is to add an after-school program" (ibid., 4).   He calls for community

educators to assist school officials and the public in understanding better the purposes of

the public CLC within the framework of community education (ibid.).

In *Transforming Schools into Community Learning Centers,* Parson explains

that public CLCs can be developed in traditional schools, much in the way that

chartered schools have been established.   Though facilities might be different across

CLCs, he does recognize some commonalities (1999, 7):

- Services are provided to the whole community in addition to focusing on the
  educational needs of the children.

- Community resources become a regular part of the instructional program.

- Community services for families and children work together in the community
  learning center to provide needed programs and services.

- People from throughout the community can gain access to technology in the
  community learning center.

- Leadership is shared among all the community stockholders.

Mission in Jeopardy

The 21ˢᵗ Century CLC Program has not become what the program architects

intended.   With much emphasis on alternative goals, such as *Goals 2000,* community

learning centers have not been able to accomplish their mission, which is to provide

four out of the thirteen programs in public schools (refer to pg. 19); and this has raised

questions on Capitol Hill.   Former Representative Steve Gunderson of Wisconsin was one of the architects for the 21ˢᵗ Century CLC Program, and states that "concentrating most of the centers in elementary and middle schools defeats the intended purpose of offering a variety of community-based training programs. Such schools…are ill-equipped to handle much beyond child care" and this makes the CLCs look like "nothing more than glorified baby-sitting" (abcnews.com, "politics," 2). Because of these grave concerns, Michael Cohen, a deputy to Education Secretary Richard Riley, was told by Rep. Bill Goodling, chairman of the House Education and Workforce Committee, that the Department of Education would need to "study the centers' effectiveness before asking for more money" to continue developing CLCs (ibid.).

Conclusion

Though the 21ˢᵗ Century CLC Program was created to further the educational opportunities of all citizens, it is not the kind of CLC system that is supported in this paper. As John Dewey declares in *Democracy and Education*, education itself cannot have a single aim. People have aims and education's task is to provide people with support in meeting their individual educational goals. The 21ˢᵗ Century CLC Program has made an effort to satisfy external aims, such as *Goals 2000*, as well as to satisfy the single aims of learners. The problem that arises is that there cannot be both compulsion and choice. One has to give way to the other.

Jewish Community Centers of Chicago

<u>Background</u>

The Jewish Community Centers of Chicago (JCCs of Chicago) is a sectarian life-long learning community learning network. The JCCs of Chicago was founded in 1903 as the Chicago Hebrew Institute when a group of Jewish community leaders in Chicago came together to discuss the need for community space for the Jewish people residing in the West Side of Chicago (JCC, "about", 1).

Over the course of one century, the JCCs of Chicago grew from one center on the West Side of Chicago to seven community centers throughout the entire Chicago metropolitan area. Each center is unique in that each reflects "the distinct personalities of the neighborhoods [that each serves] by offering a rich array of programs for children, teens, adults, and families" (ibid.). The network within which these centers exist is held together physically by a central office, electronically by a website, and spiritually by its faith. The network includes a central office, seven neighborhood centers, a center for Jewish education, a center for Jewish Arts & Letters, a center for adult education, a center for Russian senior citizens, a Yiddish Institute, a multi-service center, several camps for both summer and winter, and a resort and conference center for camping and vacationing (JCC, "home",1).

<u>Early Childhood Education (Birth to Five Years)</u>

The underlying philosophy of the JCCs of Chicago early childhood education program is the belief in experiential learning (JCC, "infants", 1).

Early Childhood programs are based on the belief that children learn about the world in different ways and at various rates, and that when children have positive experiences in preschool, they develop positive attitudes toward kindergarten and beyond. Through fun and enriching play and problem-solving activities, children gain the basic skills necessary for future achievement—academic, social, emotional and spiritual.

Another interesting aspect of the philosophy is the combination of learning and Jewish values. The program integrates learning and values so that "children become familiar with Jewish values and develop an appreciation for...rich Jewish heritage" (ibid.) This is done through a variety of learning situations, such as in-classroom learning, family programs with parents, and the celebration of religious holidays.

The learning environment at JCCs is created based upon current research in the fields of cognitive development and human growth. The early childhood program is child-centered and focuses specifically on children positively interacting with the environment. The program revolves around a "daily schedule that provides social and cognitive stimulation, creative and structured activities, and individual and group experiences—all designed to allow children to develop skills and abilities at their own pace, without pressure, in warm and stimulating surroundings" (ibid.).

The Early Childhood Learning Center is divided into seven areas. Though not explicitly stated on the website, each center focuses on one of the seven multiple intelligences that Howard Gardner discusses in *Intelligence Reframed*. The Circle

Time Area promotes both linguistic and musical intelligences. The language activities "provide opportunities to learn new concepts, use social skills and appreciate literature" (JCC, "infants/classroom", 1). The music activities are equally important because music "creates a foundation for math, logic, abstract thinking, and it aids in the comprehension and retention of ideas" and also fosters "self-expression and confidence" (ibid.).

The Manipulative Area focuses on spatial intelligence. It contains small games, toys, puzzles, and imaginative play so children will be able to improve their muscle coordination and have the opportunity to work with spatial relationships (ibid.).

The Dress Up/Dramatic Play Area promotes the interpersonal/intrapersonal intelligences. Dramatic play allows the children to "expand their imaginations, create their own worlds, safely act out life experiences and develop social and language skills" (ibid.).

The Reading Corner is similar to the Circle Time Area in that it supports the linguistic intelligence, but unlike the Circle Time Area it focuses specifically on the connection between written symbols and ideas (ibid.).

The Block Area develops the logical-mathematical intelligence of children. Through the use of block-building, "children learn about weight, balance, space, dimension, problem solving and logical thinking, all while developing small muscle skills" (ibid.).

The Sensory Table strengthens several intelligences at once, logical-mathematical, spatial, and bodily-kinesthetic. The activities use a variety of manipulative materials, such as water, sand, rice, and beans. With these objects children learn about "volume, cause and effect and have endless possibilities for self-expression" (ibid., 2).

The Art Area also promotes several intelligences at once, such as bodily-kinesthetic, logical-mathematical, and intrapersonal. The art activities are designed to "encourage the expression of thoughts and the expansion of creativity through color, space, texture, and design" and to "expand their sensory experiences" (ibid.).

Kindergarten (Age Six)

The kindergarten programs expand upon the multiple intelligences curriculum of the early childhood program. A wide range of learning activities is offered that includes math, science, computer and music instruction, reading and language, foreign languages, gymnastics, sports, art and music, ballet, cooking, and social studies. The program is licensed by the State of Illinois and taught by certified teachers (JCC, "infants/kinder", 1-2).

Older Children (Seven to Twelve Years)

JCCs offers a variety of recreational and after-school programs for children from ages seven to twelve years. The sports and leagues include activities such as Tae Kwon Do, swimming, and basketball. In addition, each of the centers provides tutorial services for children with working parents. These tutorial centers are designed to "provide a safe, structured environment where children can participate in a variety of recreational and educational activities" while their parents are still away at work (JCC, "children," 1).

Adolescents (Thirteen to Seventeen Years)

JCCs offers a variety of recreational activities for youth. Activities include summer outings across the U.S., Canada, and Israel; the traditional summer Camp Chi; and the Maccabi Youth Games (JCC, "teens," 1).

Located in Lake Delton, Wisconsin, Camp Chi has been in operation for the last seventy-seven years offering third through twelfth graders a multitude of services and activities: air-conditioned gym & recreation center, heated pool, climbing and rappelling tower, fine arts center, water skiing and sailing site, video and radio production studio, equestrian stables, roller hockey arena, low ropes course, athletic fields, and basketball, volleyball and tennis courts (JCC, "chi," 1).

Each year the Maccabi JCC of Chicago holds an Olympic-style competition for Jewish teens of ages thirteen to sixteen. It is similar to the World Maccabi Games that are held every four years in Israel. The games bring together about one-thousand Jewish youth from around the world to compete in various sporting events such as baseball, softball, basketball, bowling, golf, and gymnastics (JCC, "teens," 1).

Adults

JCCs hosts a variety of adult programs and activities: Lectures & Discussion Groups, SeniorNet, Elederhostel, Perlstein Resort & Conference Center, The Marvin N. Stone Centre for Jewish Arts & Letters, JCC Travel, Russian Senior Center, City North Kehilla, and the JCC Chicago Yiddish Institute (JCC, "adults," 1-2).

The Lectures & Discussion Groups provides for adults interesting programs and discussion groups regarding a variety of topics, from current events or emerging social issues to movies or women's issues (ibid., 1).

SeniorNet was created for adults ages fifty and over in order to assist them with becoming more comfortable with and skilled at the use of computers (ibid.).

Elderhostel provides college level courses to seniors that focus on Jewish studies and humanities. The classes are held at the Perlstein Resort & Conference Center (ibid.).

The Perlstein Resort & Conference Center is located on Lake Blass in Delton, Wisconsin. It offers seniors and families a variety of recreational services and amenities (ibid.).

The Marvin N. Stone Centre for Jewish Arts & Letters was established as a means "to enrich, educate and inspire" Jewish adults. The Centre provides panel discussions and presentations on a variety of topics (ibid., 2).

JCC Travel is a service that provides a variety of travel programs for adults and seniors. These travel services could be a one week ship cruise to a two week Israel pilgrimage (ibid., 2).

Established in 1994, The Russian Senior Center provides "unique acculturation and affiliate opportunities for older adults from the former Soviet Union" (ibid., 2). The programs offered include the Russian language, cultural, recreational, health, educational, and social opportunities for Russian senior citizens (ibid.).

City North Kehilla was created in order "to bring together young Jewish adults as part of the Jewish community" (ibid.). It requires a membership and includes tickets to holiday events provided by the Kehilla and other annual programs (ibid.).

JCC Chicago Yiddish Institute was established in 1990 in order to provide for men and women "a weekend of hospitality and *Yiddishkeit*...dedicated to keeping the Yiddish language and culture alive" (ibid.). The Institute is held each fall at the Perlstein Resort and Conference Center with nearly one hundred or more individuals participating in lecturers and events (ibid.).

Conclusion

Though it is a sectarian learning network, the JCCs of Chicago epitomizes the concept of the public learning network that is developed later in this paper. The JCCs is held together physically by a central administrative office, electronically by a website, and spiritually by the common belief and value systems of the Jewish people.

Furthermore, each community center is unique in that each represents the character of its community.

The life-long educational program that the JCCs provides is a holistic approach toward learning that public CLCs should model. The Early Childhood Program is in alignment with current research in cognitive development and human growth and works toward the actualization of an individual's inner potential at a pace that is commensurate with his growth. In addition, the programs for youth are an important component in the process of growth-toward-self-actualization. Finally, the adult and senior citizen programs assist its elder members to stay connected with their community and contribute something of benefit to themselves and others.

Chapter 2: Community Learning Concept Contributors

Though numerous individuals have contributed to the concept of community learning, only Ivan Illich, Malcolm Knowles, Bela Banathy, James Moffett, Charles M. Reigeluth, and Robert L. Fried have been selected for discussion in this chapter. They have been chosen based upon three criteria.

1. Does the idea presented explore educational change and renewal from the greater view of the transformed society; and is the idea a new design of the educational system?

2. Does the new educational system focus on *the processes of learning*?

3. Does the new educational system call for systemic design with the design being done by participants from all aspects of the greater community? As will be revealed later in this paper, Banathy contends that those involved in systemic design should ask: a) Does the educational system serve the purposes for which it was designed? b) Does the educational system serve the people in the system? c) Does the educational system serve the other social systems?

In this chapter the term community learning network is expanded upon. In the field of education it was first introduced by Ivan Illich; however, instead of network he preferred to use the term "educational web." In his words, a network is often used to mean the designated "channels reserved to material selected by others for indoctrination, instruction, and entertainment" (1970, 110). However, a "web" implies "reticular structures for mutual access" (ibid.). In this paper, the words are used interchangeably.

Knowles, Banathy, and Reigeluth employ the term "system" when talking about a community learning network, but Banathy also uses a more specific term, "Learning Society." Fried grounds his CLC Project in the idea of "learning in community." Moffett employs the term "community learning network" throughout *The Universal Schoolhouse.* Since "network" seems to be the most common phrase these days among colleagues in "A Coalition for Self Learning," "network" or "system" is employed more often in the paper than "learning web," but the terms are used interchangeably so that when "web" is used it also means "network" or "system."

Ivan Illich

Ivan Illich in *Deschooling Society*, conceives learning without school buildings and puts forth a remarkable concept for learning: learning webs or networks. Illich defines a learning web as "reticular structures for mutual access…to the public and designed to spread equal opportunity for learning and teaching" (1970, 110). He prefers the term "web" over network because "network" is often meant "to designate the channels reserved to material selected by others for indoctrination, instruction, and entertainment" (ibid., 109-110). He identifies four kinds of networks in a learning web: Reference Services to Educational Objects, Skill Exchanges, Peer-Matching, and Reference Services to Educators-at-Large (ibid., 112-113).

Reference Services to Educational Objects

Reference Services to Educational Objects are reference services that put people in contact with resources, people, and/or organizations that are used in formal learning (ibid.). Today, the Internet is the greatest reference service tool. Illich argues that all objects within the community should serve as educational objects and that everyone should be able to have access to them at reasonable times. He opposes the idea of centering educational objects solely around school buildings or private labs and offices, often out of reach to the general public. He cites the example of current human artifacts and contends that it is difficult for people to learn anything about the objects that they use (ibid., 114-115).

In order to allow people access to educational objects, Illich calls for their liberation and the development of a public system in which they can be accessed. In his scheme, communities could either establish a community budget or provide individual vouchers to fund this system and tax incentives could be given to those businesses that provide humane apprenticeship or internship opportunities (ibid., 121-122).

- *Community Budget*: Community would fund the arrangement within the network so that it would be open to everyone at reasonable hours.
- *Limited Entitlements*: Citizens would receive vouchers that are graded according to their age which provide them access to those resources that are costly and scarce.
- *Tax Incentives*: Tax breaks would be given to those organizations or persons who provide humane conditions for internship or apprenticeship experiences for children between the ages of eight and fourteen.

Skill Exchanges

Skill Exchanges are those exchanges of skills that people have which can be taught to others (ibid., 113).   Illich argues that society currently makes skill exchanges scarce because of "the institutional requirement that those who can demonstrate them may not do so unless they are given public trust, through a certificate" (ibid., 127).   He suggests providing a community bulletin board in each community that lists the skills taught, by whom, and a contact address or phone number in order to free-up the market for skill exchanges.   For example, if Mrs. Smith wants to advertise piano lessons for children, she can do so by posting her information on a community bulletin board. Illich suggests two approaches for skill exchanges (ibid., 130):

- *Institutionalized Skill Exchanges*: Free and open skill centers for the public that are established in industrialized areas of the community in order to offer skills that are prerequisites for entering certain apprenticeships.

- *Educational Currency*: Credits that are given to everyone in the community to use for skill exchanges.   Those who would teach something would earn credits instead of "dollars."

Peer-Matching

Peer-Matching is the advertising of a skill that someone wants to learn with the hope of finding someone who is able to teach it to them (ibid., 113).   Instead of forcing children into a class based upon age, Illich suggests that children be matched based upon similar interest in an activity.   He recommends that a communications network be established in which peers are able to communicate with one another regarding similar learning interests and needs (ibid., 133).

The peer-matching system would be similar to that of the skill exchange in that "the user would identify himself by name and address and describe the activity for which he sought a peer" (ibid., 134).   Of course, Illich does not neglect the privacy issue or the abuse of information.   He proposes that the matching system "allow only pertinent printed information, plus the name and address of the inquirer, to be used" (ibid., 136).

Professional Educators

Reference Services to Educators-at-Large are directories that list professionals, paraprofessionals, or freelancers in a given field. It includes the contact names and addresses as well as a description of the services that are provided (ibid., 113). One example of this is a common directory among alternative educators, *Guidebook & Directory of Consultants for Creating Learning Communities*, that is published by "A Coalition for Self Learning."

Illich envisions a system in which master-teachers are no longer confined to a school building, but would offer their services over the community bulletin board. As a community becomes "de-schooled" the demand of parents and youth for master-teachers to serve as guides increases. In today's hectic world, it is very difficult for parents to offer much of their time toward guidance and learning. Thus, he suggests establishing a learning web that provides professional guides who are well versed in child psychology, sociology, and pedagogy and are able to assist families with developing learning plans for children (ibid., 141).

Professional educators would also participate in the design of the learning web. These people "would have to demonstrate genius at keeping themselves, and others, out of people's way, at facilitating encounters among students, skill models, educational leaders, and educational objects" (ibid., 142). Thus, administrators would no longer be administering people, but instead would be administering the community's learning web, allowing the "pedagogues" to "help the student to find the path which for him could lead fastest to his goal" (ibid., 143).

Malcolm Knowles

Malcolm Knowles in *Creating Lifelong Learning Communities* (1983) and *Self-Directed Learning* (1975), provides a conceptual framework within which all social systems are viewed as systems of learning resources; and contends that a "systems theory approach" to learning is required for designing a new educational framework. He makes reference to several key thinkers, such as Ludwig von Bertlanffy, John Hayman, Jr. and Frijtof Capra, all of whom argue that systems theory is more appropriate for dealing with the complexities of today's world than the Cartesian-Newtonian scientific method (1983, 4).

Furthermore, he purports that a systemic view of education transforms the purpose of school from that of a "provider of information" to that of a developer of a learner's skills with the objective of engaging the individual "effectively in collaborative self-directed inquiry in self-actualizing directions" (ibid., 10).

The learning skills Knowles identifies for a self-directed lifelong learning resource system include (ibid., 10):

- Ability to think in different ways and maintain one's curiosity.
- Ability to perceive of oneself in an objective manner and be open-minded about constructive feedback.
- Ability to diagnose oneself in regards to learning needs and life roles in society.
- Ability to design one's own learning objectives and performance outcomes.

- Ability to identify various kinds of learning resources for carrying out one's own learning program.

- Ability to design strategies for using those resources.

- Ability to implement one's learning plan in a systemic and sequential manner.

- Ability to collect evidence of one's own learning and to evaluate that evidence in reference to learning objectives and performance outcomes.

Knowles further states that a model of a lifelong learning resource system is based upon several assumptions of learning (ibid., 4-5):

- Learning is a lifelong process.

- Learning involves active inquiry with the motivation to learn to be found in the learner's own curiosities.

- Learning is guided by the educational purpose to develop within each learner the competencies necessary for fulfilling life roles in society.

- Learning is focused on the learner and programs are developed around him, that is it considers his individual learning styles, intelligences, and readiness to learn.

- Learning involves connecting learners with the necessary learning resources.

- Learning involves helping people make the transition from a state of dependence to a state of independence and self-directed learning.

- Learning is improved in quality via interactions with others.

- Learning is more effective if it is guided by process rather than by content.

Knowles continues his discussion on lifelong learning and provides four steps for developing a lifelong learning resource system. These include identifying the necessary learning resources of a community, categorizing these resources, establishing a structure that helps to make policy and administer the learning system, and designing the lifelong learning system (ibid., 5-6).

Knowles' process design of a lifelong learning resource system involves broadening and deepening the skills necessary for self-directed learning, such as providing self-directed learning in increments at each stage of the learning process, diagnosing learning needs or competency-development needs, translating needs into learning objectives, identifying learning resources and experiences for accomplishing learning objectives, implementing the learning program, and finally, assessing one's learning in terms of the objectives (ibid., 6).

The Learning Process

Knowles' learning system process begins with an individual entering into one of the learning centers in the community and then receiving an assessment of his ability to plan and carry out a self-directed learning project. The learner then begins consulting with an educational diagnostician who assists the learner with deciding on a life role[2] at the appropriate stage of development. He suggests that the diagnostician "engage with the learner in a set of performance assessments to determine what knowledge, understandings, skills, attitudes, and values the learner needs to acquire in order to achieve the level of performance specified by the competency model" (ibid., 7).

---

[2] Refer to Table 1, page 44.

Once consultations with the diagnostician have been completed, the learner meets with an educational planning consultant.   Through the use of a community learning resource data bank, the educational consultant assists the learner with developing an individualized curriculum, which Knowles refers to as a "learning contract" (ibid.).   The learning contract, as explained in *Self-Directed Learning*, contains five elements: a) learning objectives, b) learning resources and strategies, c) evidence of accomplishment, d) criteria and means of validating evidence, and e) time frame (ibid., 62).

Finally, the learner goes to the learning resources in the community, alone or with peers, and carries out his learning plan.   He may be assigned to teachers who have knowledge or skills in a specialized field and learn from them, or work within a general learning environment on various subjects taught by a single teacher.

After the learner has completed his learning plan, he returns to the center for a "re-diagnosis" and evaluation of his learning contract.   He determines if he 1) has met his learning objectives, 2) is satisfied with his learning, and 3) should make any changes in his learning plan (ibid., 7).

Table 1. Competencies for Performing Life Roles (Knowles 1983, 11)

Roles	Competencies
Learner	Reading, writing, computing, conceptualizing, imagining, inquiring, aspiring, diagnosing, planning, getting help, evaluating.
Being a self (with unique self identity)	Self-analyzing, sensing, goal-building, objectivizing, value-clarifying, expressing, accepting, being authentic.
Friend	Loving, empathizing, listening, collaborating, sharing, helping, giving constructive feedback, supporting.
Citizen	Caring, participating, leading, decision-making, acting, "conscientizing," discussing, having perspective (historical and cultural), global citizen.
Family member	Maintaining health, planning, managing, helping, sharing, buying, saving, loving, taking responsibility.
Worker	Career planning, using technical skills, accepting supervision, giving supervision, getting along with people, cooperating, planning, delegating, managing.
Leisure-time user	Knowing resources, appreciating the arts and humanities, performing, playing, relaxing, reflecting, planning, risking.

Bela Banathy

Bela Banathy in *Systems Design of Education*, develops an educational framework that he refers to as a "Learning Society."   In developing this framework, he employs his own method of systemic design that has taken him at least thirty years to formulate.   He argues that in contrast with the traditional scientific Cartesian-Newtonian model which atomistically analyzes problems, the systems design approach is far better in seeking to understand the crisis in today's educational system because it takes a holistic approach toward "problem-situations" (ibid., 11-12).   Furthermore, systems design helps a community address the following questions (ibid.): Is the system doing what it was designed to do?   Is the system serving the people who are using the system?   Is the system serving the greater society that created the system?

In designing a new educational system, Banathy focuses on transformation and not reformation.   Transformation is used in "times of accelerating and dynamic societal changes, when a new stage is unfolding in societal evolution" (ibid., 15).   Reformation is applied when "improving existing systems" (ibid.).   Because of the current educational dilemma and evidence of societal change, Banathy asserts that today's educational systems should be **transformed** and not reformed.   This requires people to "jump out from the system," and explore the elements that are transforming society and design a new educational system that is based upon a vision and ideas of future learning (ibid., 15-16).

As help to future designers of educational systems, Banathy provides a vision, ideas, and design of an alternative learning system.   He envisions a *learning society* that aspires toward *paideia*—"a society in which learning, fulfillment, and becoming truly human are the primary goals" (ibid., 124).

He identifies certain values for this new learning system. He purports that the individual and the global system of humanity's values are the two absolute values and that social systems should work to serve both. Two types of social systems that should be arranged around these values include learning and human development systems (ibid., 126). He gives great credence to human potential and argues that the most important resource is "the uniqueness and the unique potential and creativity residing in the individual, in the family, and in our various social systems" (ibid.). These are supported by the values that people ascribe to human rights as well as the right to learn and think freely. He contends that self-actualization is of utmost importance to society and is "the highest value" for people (ibid.). Banathy does not view the individual as the ultimate source of being. Rather, he values the development and maintenance of "creative and cooperative interpersonal and social relationships" in society (ibid.). He argues that the highest value of all these for a "Learning Society" is that of nurturing learning and human development (ibid.).

In addition to providing a vision statement and a set of core values, Banathy develops an example set of core ideas about the new learning system. Though vision and values are important, he asserts that the core ideas are "the 'stuff' of which the image is made" (ibid., 126). The ideas that he develops are arranged into three sets: functions and purposes, learner and learning, and design guidance.

Functions and Purposes

The main function and purpose for every community is to design itself into a learning society and to include subordinate functions and purposes, such as (ibid., 127),

1. Aspire toward providing for individuals and the systems to which they belong learning environments that will assist them in attaining the competence required to function properly in the larger societal system and be empowered to control their own destinies.

2. Co-evolve learning systems and human development with the greater societal system and allow them to lead societal evolution.

3. Nurture all forms of existential experience. These include the following domains of life: social, cultural, ethical, economic, physical, mental, spiritual, intellectual, aesthetic, and moral.

4. Integrate content, learning experiences, and human development into the main stream of educational experience.

5. Develop the necessary structures and networks to allow individuals to learn on a continuous basis about organizational learning and design.

6. Provide for learners a learning network that has arrangements, resources, and opportunities for them to actualize their true potentials.

Learner and Learning

Banathy grounds learning in the realm of the individual, recognizing the cognitive and emotional aspects of the learner and the place that learning has in relationship to those aspects (ibid., 127-128).

1. Learning has no boundaries; learning and human development are continuous.

2. It is the instinctive nature of all human beings to learn and become competent at the skills necessary for properly functioning in their respective societies.

3. All competent people are capable of self-directed learning and taking on responsibility.

4. All persons learn best if their unique abilities are recognized, respected and nurtured by society.

5. Learning can only begin with individual intrinsic inspiration and motivation to learn.

6. People learn best when they are learning new things, new insights and acquiring new skills.

7. Mastering and applying new skills in "real life" situations allows people to develop self-confidence.

8. All learners learn differently. They learn in different ways, at different rates, and at different times; thus, learning environments should be constructed around individual learners in order to address learning differences properly.

Design Guides

In designing an educational system, Banathy proposes the following design guides for communities. He views the entire community as one large educational resource where various sectors of the society are integrated and working together for the benefit of individual learners (ibid., 128).

1. Learning and human development should focus around the individual learner.

2. Learning should consist of knowledge, understanding, skills, dispositions, sensitivities, values, and methods of knowing and thinking.

3. Aspects and requirements of the transformational society should serve as the ultimate resource for choosing, categorizing, and planning the content of learning and human development.

4. Trust between learner and those involved in the learning system are of utmost importance for maintaining a sustainable learning environment.

5. All systems and situations within the societal system have the possibility of serving as resources for learning.

6. Systems integration of many of the social and human services already provided by the societal subsystems can create a comprehensive system of learning and human development; thus magnifying the educational and self-actualizing benefits that a community can offer.

The previously stated core ideas allow for an image of the new educational system to be created. In developing his example of an image, Banathy addresses the system's relationship with society and other systems, the main function of the system, the scope of learning, the organization of the system, kinds of interventions into the system, and resources that are to be used by learners in the system. Table 2 and Figure 2 demonstrate Banathy's image of a "Learning Society."

Table 2. Banathy's Image of a "Learning Society" (ibid., 129-130)

Image Markers	Image Description
Relationship with Society	Education should reflect and interpret the society as well as shape the society through co-evolutionary interactions, as a future-creating, innovative and open system.
Relationship with Other Systems	Education should be coordinated with other social and human service systems, integrating learning and human development.
Main Function	Education should provide resources, arrangements, and lifelong experiences for the full development of all individuals and society.
Scope of Learning	Education should embrace all domains of human and societal existence, including the socio-cultural, ethical, moral, economic/occupational, physical/mental/spiritual, political, scientific/technological, and aesthetic.
Organizational Imperative	Education should be organized around the learning experience level; arrangements should be made in the environment of the learner by which to master the learning task.
Types of Intervention	A variety of learning types should be employed: self-directed, other-directed, individually supported group learning, social and organizational learning, all employed to enhance individual and social learning.
Resources	The large reservoir of learning resources and arrangements available should be used in order to support learning.

Figure 2. Model of Banathy's Systems Complex of the "Learning Society" (ibid., 116)

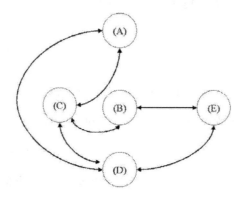

A= Governance System

B= Learners' System

C= Resources, Information, Planning, and Arrangement System

D= Resource Acquisition and Control System

E= Learning Territories and Resources Systems

In Figure 2, Banathy recognizes five systems within the societal system that contribute to the learning experience. The learner (system B) is at the center with systems (A), (C), (D), and (E) revolving around him. He outlines for each system the goals, functions, entities, relationships, and position within the learning system. An overview of these subsystems is provided below and on the following pages.

Governance System (A)

The goal of the governance system is to "ensure that each and every member of the community has easy and organized access to resources that nurture learning and human development" (ibid., 115). It does this through various functions: (a) the creation of institutions that foster the development, allocation, and use of learning resources; (b) the establishment of financial and political entities to support (a); (c) the creation of policies that govern (a) and (b); (d) the creation of monitoring and management systems for the system complex; and (e) the maintenance of the interaction with the greater community (ibid., 117). Furthermore, the key entities that exist to implement these functions include institutionalized arrangements, policies, financial resources, and people (ibid.).

The main relationship that System (A) has with Systems (C) and (D) is a direct relationship. It funds and guides (C) and (D); and through (C) and (D), guidance and support are provided to (B) and (E). Therefore, System (A) exists only to serve and support the learning experience (ibid.).

Learners' System (B)

The key entity of System (B) is the learner, and all other systems are coordinated with him and serve him (ibid., 118).   The learner's goal is to "acquire knowledge, understanding, and competence; develop attitudes, values, and sensitivities; and through all these develop his/her full potential" (ibid., 117).

In order for the learner to develop to his full potential, Systems (C) and (E) support and nurture his personal growth.   Specifically, this means assisting the learner with establishing learning goals, planning and designing one's course of study in cooperation with System (C), using learning resources appropriately, mastering certain tasks, and learning to evaluate the mastery of those tasks (ibid., 117).

Learning Resources, Information, Planning, and Arrangement System (C)

System (C) is about information and assistance and is directly related to the learner, those involved in governing the learning system, and those involved in assisting the learner to identify and use learning resources (ibid., 118).

The overall goal of System (C) is to "respond to the learner's requirements and facilitate learning by the arrangement of the use of resources, opportunities, and situations that are available in the Learning Territories and Resources Systems (E) (ibid., 118).   To achieve this goal, certain functions are necessary.   These functions include assisting the learner with developing a curriculum plan, providing information for the learner on the available learning resources in the community, making that information readily available to the learner as well as information on planning a self-directed learning program, maintaining a tracking system of the learning resources that are used by the learner, and providing continuous advice and assistance to the learner regarding his learning program (ibid., 117).

The Resource Acquisition and Control System (D)

In order to ensure the system acts efficiently and effectively, a management system is established. This requires putting into place learning territories and resources, establishing governing policies and regulations for resource acquisition and utilization, providing "caretakers" for System (D), and maintaining strong channels with the learning territories and resource systems as well as the system that deals with learning resources, information, planning, and arrangement (ibid., 119).

The goal of management is to assist the learner in identifying and using the learning resources and supervise the execution of policies that are established for the use of learning resources (ibid.). Specifically, this means providing a registration system for all learning resources coming into the educational system, developing the resources and resource territories, ensuring that resources are made available to all learners, supervising and managing the use of learning resources, and maintaining effective communication channels between all the systems (ibid.).

The Learning Territories and Resources Systems (E)

The learning territories and resources systems are the "most salient partners of the learner" and "include people, materials, arrangements, situations, and opportunities for learning and human development" (ibid., 119). The goal of this system is to provide for the learner the means and methods in which learning and human development can be facilitated. The system makes readily available to the learner tools that display and maintain the learning resources as well as allow access to those resources (ibid.). System (E) has a direct and accommodating relationship with System (B) and is coordinated with System (D) (ibid., 120).

James Moffett

James Moffett in *The Universal Schoolhouse*, expands upon the learning "web" concept that Illich proposes in *Descshooling Society*, but grounds the idea within spirituality. Despite his spiritual slant, he proposes that education be conceived in terms of societal transformation and that the system be open to all those persons who want to use it.

He envisions the "universal schoolhouse" as a decentralized system that integrates many public services of the community in order to 1) systemically address societal problems at the root cause, 2) promote an open system of education, and 3) promote a morally democratic society. It is funded on a community level. Monies go directly to members of the community and organizations who are able to serve as models, mentors, or tutors for teaching a particular skill or subject. In cases where horizontal equity does not exist, federal or state funds are provided. Even though much funding comes from the public coffers, the need for a community, state, or national oversight committee is not required. Moffett foresees each community maintaining an electronic bulletin board that provides consumer information on teachers, mentors, or tutors.

Systemic Problem Solving

Moffett argues that problems cannot be solved piecemeal—they have to be addressed systemically. Thus, he proposes that public services be integrated into the educational system in order to address many problems at once, and this does not have to occur through bureaucratic channels; it can be addressed via the learning experiences of individuals.   For example, Moffett suggests allowing university students studying to become teachers to serve as teacher-trainees in daycare centers for low-income families (1994, 295).

<u>Open System of Education</u>

For Moffett, an open system of education is also an integrated one.   In such a system each community reorganizes learning around individual learners, and this includes reorganizing organizations, resources, people, and methods of learning. Moffett cites several ways systems can be integrated together that not only address societal problems at the root cause but also provide for an open and diversified educational system.   Furthermore, he contends that business organizations can be part of the learning experience by opening their doors to apprenticeships, internships, or tours and other visitation purposes (ibid., 297-298).

Moffett also calls for shifting capital from the symptoms to the direct problems, decentralizing "taxation so that more of it can be kept in the urban and rural communities to set up the comprehensive educational networks that get at social ills right on site" (ibid., 321-322).   In addition, it would take more than property taxes to properly fund a community learning network, sales tax and perhaps income tax would go toward funding the network; and in cases of horizontal inequity, federal taxes could be used.   He sees the federal government's role as helpful but limited.   He suggests that the higher the level of government the more it should play an "informing role" in order to assist localities with knowing what is happening in other areas of the nation (ibid., 324).   Furthermore, the federal government should serve as a "watchdog" so that municipalities or other factions within communities do not abuse funds or people (ibid.).

If government's role is to provide the financial base and support but not to interfere in learning content and teaching methodology, then a very important question to ask is, "Who monitors the community learning network and how?" In Moffett's scheme, the community members themselves, with assistance from the municipality, monitor the community network. Because of the advances in technology, it is now possible to provide an electronic community bulletin board listing teachers, classes, resources, and additional people who are involved with sustaining the learning system.

First, each community would have a community website specifically for the network. The municipality or partner university would maintain this website, such as in the case of the Virginia Tech Blacksburg Electronic Village (in the interest of moral democracy, a community would not wish to place such a site into the hands of private interests). The site would contain lists for classes, teachers, mentors, tutors, educational partners, internships, apprenticeships, and resource pages with links to important resource sites (ibid., 318-319).

Second, the teachers and people involved in the educational network would receive funds for the work that they do. This is very different from a voucher system. For Moffett, a voucher system is not a solution because people only have "a gross choice among schools all complying with the same governmental policy, none of which can possibly offer what a community learning network can arrange" (ibid., 320).

Third, the things that these teachers and/or mentors do could be done in public or private facilities, such as a renovated school building, an art studio, or a home. In the case of small children, Moffett is quick to note that "self-contained sites better suit young children, who need much adult supervision and cannot get around much on their own" (ibid., 231).

Fourth, instead of relying on government to maintain the reliability of the network, the educational consumers themselves would run it by posting consumer guides on the site. Moffett believes that "a citizenry of toughly trained consumers thinking for themselves will of itself play a role of discouraging business abuse and encouraging socially and sound investments" (ibid., 320-321).

Finally, Moffett contends that courses should be designed around individual learners and a variety of methods and applications should be utilized. Individual learners would consult with professionally trained advisors or counselors for developing learning plans, such as setting goals and objectives for learning. Once the plans are designed, the learners would go to learning centers within the community to implement the plans, which would be followed-up and reviewed with the same counselors or advisors. Furthermore, various learning methods would be available to learners in implementing their plans. This could include spontaneous ways of learning (such as collaborating), deliberate learning methods (such as experimenting), concentric learning arenas (such as a classroom), rippling (an informal tutorial method that transmits knowledge and skills from more experienced individuals to learners), tutoring and coaching, apprenticing and interning, visiting, community service, playing games, therapy, practicing the arts, spiritual disciplines, home-schooling, and self-teaching (ibid., 160-200).

Moral Democratic Society

Moffett argues that compulsory unification of opinion does not create a morally democratic society, and he is very critical of the current state of affairs. Even though compulsory attendance at a designated location such as a school building might have been practical during the early days of industrialized America, today it is an impediment toward the creation of an enlightened electorate—It "has resulted in a populace that is currently throwing democracy away…*Making* people learn, and making them learn certain things in certain ways, teaches them to abide by decisions from above instead of learning to think for themselves" (ibid., 5-6).

In order to create a morally democratic society, Moffett champions the idea of personal development as the "aim of education" (ibid. 6-7). He contends that education should focus on personal development and that people should learn to participate in democracy, not be taught what it is. "Freedom can be proclaimed by legislating it," he argues, "but it can be realized only by educating for it" (ibid., 15). Furthermore, he purports that only a metaphysical framework of education will put "morality" into democracy. This can only occur by awakening the "moral and spiritual nature of a person…to a degree commensurate with the development of the person's intellect and will" (ibid., 25). In other words, one learns the virtues of society by living and learning them throughout life, starting from an early age; and this contributes to the sustainability of the democratic ideals upon which all democratic societies stand.

Charles M. Reigeluth

Charles Reigeluth (1991) for four months in 1983 worked with a small team of researchers, practitioners, parents, and teachers on the systemic design of a new educational system for their community.   They called this new system a "Third-Wave Educational System," borrowing the term "third-wave" from Alvin Toffler's, *The Third Wave*.

The Third Wave Educational System that they developed is based upon the following assumptions about education (Reigeluth 1991, 201, 203-206, 215-220):

1. The educational system should reflect the needs of an information society in the twenty-first century.

2. People learn at different rates.

3. Learning should be centered on the learner.

4. Community is an important learning resource.

5. Teachers serve as guides for learners.

6. Free market mechanisms assure educational quality.

7. Government serves best by acting as a partner in education.

Assumption 1: Education Should Reflect the Needs of an Information Society

One of the characteristics of an information society is the mass of information that is scrutinized, summarized, and categorized for use by information providers and seekers.   Because of the overwhelming amount of information in today's world, people need to know how to get the information that they want and determine which information is reliable and necessary.   Thus, the educational system should reflect this need and focus on *learning* so people can learn how to learn in an information society (ibid., 203).   Furthermore the educational system should make available "well designed resources (including interactive computer and videodisc systems), peer tutors, projects, and learning centers" in order to "convey most of the skills and knowledge" of an information society (ibid., 202-203).

Assumption 2: People Learn at Different Rates

It is now established in the field of education that people learn at different rates and in different ways; however, current curricula in many schools are still designed for *en-masse* education.   Reigeluth contends that the system *teaches* "a fixed amount of content in a fixed amount of time, and then compares the students with each other by giving A's and F's…It is as if the current educational system were designed more for selection than for learning" (ibid., 203).   In a third-wave society this should not be so. In any learning society the system "must allow time to vary so that achievement can be held constant at a mastery level" (ibid.).   A personalized education should be made available for everyone in the learning community (ibid.).

Assumption 3: Learning Should Focus on the Learner

Because people learn at different rates and in different ways, learning should focus on the learner.   Reigeluth refers to Howard Gardner's work with multiple intelligences, and asserts that learning goals should be personalized and go beyond the intellectual development of the child, to "extend to the child's physical, social, moral, emotional, and psychological development" (ibid., 204).   Reigeluth's personalized curricular scheme is based upon the work of cognitive psychologists, such as Piaget, Erikson, and Gardner since they all subscribe to the notion that learning methods should be in alignment with certain stages of life.

Assumption 4: Community Is an Important Learning Resource

Reigeluth recognizes that in an information society learning occurs more often outside of the school than within it (ibid., 203). He envisions a learning society in which community resources are identified, categorized, and made available to the greater community as "learning centers" (ibid., 212). A learning center is an educational enterprise that provides for learners specialized expertise, learning resources, and instruction in thinking and higher-order skills within a focused area of instruction (ibid.). Teacher-guides assist the learners in developing an educational program that "represents a good progression of such higher-order skills instruction" (ibid.). The focus areas that he identifies could be in the more traditional, discipline-oriented fields such as history or biology. They also could be in thematic, cross-disciplinary, problem-oriented fields such as environmental pollution or world food supply (ibid.).

Assumption 5: Teachers Serve as Guides for Learners

In a third-wave educational system, the role of the teacher is transformed from that of a lecturer to that of a guide. Since knowledge is stored in databases and is provided to learners in various contexts via multimedia and/or interactive computer assisted learning devices, the teacher can assist learners by facilitating their learning instead of lecturing to them about facts (ibid., 203).

Guides, as Reigeluth refers to them, work individually with learners in small groups called "clusters" over a three-year period in one of the stages of life (ibid., 204). With the assistance of computer-based advisement and management tools, guides work with parents and children in developing personalized curricula.   Instead of teaching, "cluster guides" take their small group of learners to learning centers throughout the learning network or the community, and the specialists at those centers are the ones who engage the children in the various learning activities that they provide (ibid., 207).

Assumption 6: Free Market Mechanisms Assure Educational Quality

Reigeluth ties quality assurance of a third-wave educational system to free market mechanisms (ibid., 205-206).   One of the elements of his system is the cluster. Instead of schools, school districts charter learning clusters to those persons who are certified as guides.   A cluster is an organization of teaching professionals or guides, similar to medical or legal professional organizations (ibid., 205).   These clusters have control over their organization and curricula.   Parents freely choose individual guides who belong to a cluster, and clusters can, if they wish, limit the number of students they accept.   For Reigeluth, the optimal cluster size is four to ten guides, assistants, any number of students, and a master guide (ibid.).

In order to attract students, the clusters advertise via an electronic community bulletin board.   The advertisements include specifics such as information about the guides, the age focus of a guide's group, and the number of students a guide will accept (ibid., 206).   Parents then choose clusters for their children based upon information that is made available by a district-wide consumer report, similar to that of the Better

Business Bureau's reports, as well as by word-of-mouth. The district's consumer support office also has diagnostic testing and interviews in order to help parents choose the right cluster for their children (ibid., 205).

In order to assure that clusters are relevant to the needs of the community, a special budgeting system is initiated that is in alignment with free market thought. After a cluster has been formed, it will receive an initial budget from the school district. The budget is solely dependent upon *the demand for the cluster's guides*, not the income of each individual guide.   Thus, if the demand for individual guides increases, the budget for the following fiscal year increases; and if demand falls, the budget too declines.   In addition, a guide's full-time income is directly related to the guides' decision on how to spend the budget, and each guide's salary is then adjusted for the percentage of work the guide is doing, e.g. the number of students.   According to Reigeluth, this provides an incentive for guides to help one another perform better, and is in alignment with a more humane form of competition and cooperation.   Also, if a cluster is not performing well, incubation policies are created in order to transform old clusters into new clusters without the risk of losing guides (ibid., 206).

Free market mechanisms are also at play in funding learning centers. Learning centers play an important role in assisting clusters, but are independent from them.   Any facility that is recognized by the school district as a legitimate place for public learning can be designated as a community learning center, e.g. a private or public museum, a corporation, or someone's home for piano lessons.   The budgets of these learning centers are based upon private and public funds, such as a district pass system.   All learners in the community receive a certain number of passes that can be used at these centers.   The more passes a center receives, the more funds it will get in the following fiscal year to meet user demand (ibid., 207).   In addition, people can receive passes by volunteering to teach or work at a learning center.   For example, a high school student could receive passes for tutoring five-year olds, and those passes could then be used at a learning center of his choice (ibid., 208).

Assumption 7: Government Serves Best as a Partner of Education

Free market mechanisms in a third-wave educational system assure the quality of education that is made available to learners, but the free market cannot act alone.   It requires a faithful and active relationship with government at the local, state, and federal levels.   Several ways exist in which government can act in assuring that free market mechanisms work well.   First, the government can make available public space for learning centers, such as renovated school buildings or community centers (ibid., 207).

Second, government plays a very important role in creating the community network by identifying, categorizing, and making available information on community learning resources.   As stated previously, each school district would provide a "consumer support office" for parents to use in choosing the right cluster for their children.   This office would also maintain consumer reports on clusters, guides, centers, and the consumer report office's activities.   In addition, the office would provide diagnostic testing and interviewing in order to assist parents in placing their children in the most appropriate clusters (ibid., 205).   A final important feature of the office would be the employment of citizen ownership.   Volunteer parents, not paid bureaucrats, would operate the facility that would be funded by a "permanent fixed budget" from the school district; thus assuring a system of checks-and-balances for both parties (ibid., 219).

Third, funding of learning centers, clusters, and passes would come initially from public sources; thus, government has a very important role in establishing funding criteria, such as requiring training and certification for guides. For learning centers, Reigeluth envisions a Learning Center Management Organization that would be responsible for surveying cluster needs and prioritizing them, contracting new learning centers and guides, training learning center directors and providing professional development support for centers, and distributing funds to learning centers for the amount that each center uses (ibid., 218).

In addition to establishing funding criteria, school districts would assist clusters with the accounting, reports, and logistical aspects, but each cluster decides how to spend its budget (ibid., 217). Pedagogy is left to the guides and volunteer teachers at the centers in order to ensure intellectual freedom. Fiscal accountability is left to government in order to serve as a check against the misuse of public funds. Thus, even though a cluster receives public funds and guides decide their own salaries, increasing salaries too much could take away from other cluster activities which could displease parents and lower the cluster's enrollment and decrease its budget for the following year (ibid.).

Reigeluth discusses other details about the logistics of the learning centers. However, for purposes of this treatise, discussion will be limited to his own summary of the characteristics of a third-wave educational system (ibid., 207-208).

1. Teachers are guides who, in cooperation with the child's parents, motivate, advise, and manage a child's education for 3 to 5 years.

2. Educational resources (including well-designed materials, peer tutors, projects, discussion groups, learning centers, and resource people) are used to effect most of the learning.

3. There are no traditional "classes," but each child has individual goals, and a unique combination of resources and approaches is prescribed to reach those goals.

4. Guides work cooperatively within an educational cluster with about 4 to 9 other guides, including a master guide.

5. The master guide sets the school climate and philosophy, hires guides and assistants, provides professional development for guides and assistants, and provides direction and leadership for the whole cluster.

6. After a trial period, parents are free to request to move their child to another available guide and cluster if they are not satisfied with their child's progress. Hence, individual guides and clusters are very accountable for what they do or don't do, and they have considerable incentive to work with parents.

7. Guides have a great financial incentive to cooperate and work together for the success of the whole cluster.

8. Guides can send children to learning centers of various kinds to receive the best available instruction in selected focus areas.

Robert L. Fried

Robert Fried from 1973 through 1975 worked with eight small communities in New Hampshire in the development of the Community Learning Center Project.   It was an informal, non-credit, tuition-free community-based adult education program that was supported by a grant from the U.S. Department of Health, Education, and Welfare's Improvement of Post-secondary Education and sponsored by the University System of New Hampshire's School of Continuing Studies.   In his dissertation, *Toward Learning In Community* (1976), and his monograph, *Learning in Community: An Empowerment Approach* (1980), he discusses the CLC project and the implications of self-created/self-directed learning for "learning-in-community."

In this paper, the term "learning-in-community" is employed instead of "community education" in order to distinguish between "community-based learning processes" and "the delivery of educational programs."   Fried is credited here in making such a distinction in *Toward Learning In Community* (1976, v).

In exploring the idea of "learning-in-community," Fried also presses to explore four philosophical issues: education vs. learning; de-schooling society vs. educationally re-endowing society; value, preservation, and enrichment of small communities; and empowerment vs. delivery of services (1976, v).   It is by exploring these issues that Fried assists community-based educators in better understanding the benefits of self-created/self-directed learning for the sustainability of communities.

The first issue that Fried addresses is Education vs. Learning.   He asks, "How can learning—as a process of people seeking to enhance their lives by acquiring knowledge, skill, and understanding—come out from under the control of institutionalized education?"   In answering this question, he distinguishes between education and learning.   Education in modern society has come to mean some bit of knowledge, a commodity, that one "gets" for the betterment of oneself in society, not something one "does" for the betterment of himself and society (1976, 62).   He views learning as "a *process*, one that is largely within the control of the person seeking knowledge…a process of people seeking to enhance their lives by acquiring knowledge, skill, and understanding" (ibid., 62, 64).   He describes the learning process as people defining their own learning needs, developing their own learning structures and settings, and benefiting from a reciprocal learning process that is controlled by learners for the benefit of learners (ibid., 64-65).   Furthermore, in developing oneself to one's fullest potential, he contends that "it is important that learning experiences allow people to express those different interests and ideas freely and fully, so that self-development doesn't come to mean that everybody has to 'develop' themselves the same way" (ibid., Appendix E, 7).

The second issue that Fried addresses is De-schooling vs. Educational Re-endowing.   He argues that while there might have been a time when "schooling" was important to produce a literate electorate and skilled-labor for an industrialized age in western society, the world-wide monopolization of "society's access to and recognition of learning" by schools has also created various culturally harmful effects (1976, 67). For instance, in the nation of Tanzania, much of the traditional knowledge is being lost.

He refers to former President Nyrere who describes an Africa that was rich in traditions and re-enforced learning by doing, such as with the occupation of farming. However, in today's Africa formal education has caused the young to lose their basic knowledge of the earth as a result of it being substituted for formal knowledge that is not applicable to African life (ibid., 68).

In order to reverse the harmful effects of formalized schooling, Fried calls for "educational re-endowment" instead of Illich's "de-schooling." He states that de-schooling implies "the tearing down of schools or the dismissal of skilled and dedicated teachers;" whereas educational re-endowment means "*re-legitimizing* the community with an educative role...*re-endowing*...citizens with their right and value in contributing to each other's learning as well as to that of their children, regardless of how much formal schooling these citizens received" (italics added for emphasis, ibid., 69). Furthermore, the schools themselves must break the monopolization of learning and access to learning resources (ibid.).

Fried contends that one way to re-endow society and allow schools to break the monopolization of learning is to conceive of learning within three contexts: school context, laboratory-studio-work context, and the community seminar context. The school context involves "systematic, planned instruction" that occurs within the school (ibid., 70). This planning is done with educational professionals who have been trained in a specific discipline of knowledge, are well accustomed to teaching pedagogy, and have the ability to assist learners with designing and initiating a learning plan. The laboratory-studio-work context is learning that occurs within the community itself and assists with developing "problem-solving skills." This kind of learning could occur in a factory, art studio, hospital, library, or science or industrial laboratory (ibid.). The community seminar context is learning that occurs at seminars presented by various people within the community. The purpose of the seminar is to promote "reflective exploration of community issues" and "create opportunities for people of all ages and groupings to examine and discuss issues of mutual concern" (ibid., 70-71).

Value, Preservation, and Enrichment of Small Communities is the third issue addressed by Fried. One of his biggest concerns when he developed the CLC Project was community. He cites several critics who observe that the path toward suburbanization and urbanization has done much to disintegrate community life. He believes that the challenges we face in saving community life are exploring "new contexts for social cohesion among individuals and new concepts of community life" and examining "the viability of existing small communities" (1976, 81).

For his CLC Project, Fried chose to work with communities with populations of three thousand residents or less. In each community a "core group" that was made of a cross-section of adult learners from the community formed to "build...programs of informal learning activities around not only the needs and desires of local residents, but upon their [core group members'] talents and expertise as well" (ibid., 83). The groups had to be self-reliant and think of ways to organize, fund, and implement their learning programs.

Fried concluded that the value, preservation, and enrichment of small communities supported the idea that "community-based learning is a personally meaningful one" (ibid., 84-85). The issues that the participants engaged in were communal, the people with or from whom they learned were from a cross-section of the community, and other communities tended to respond to the activities by beginning their own community programs (ibid.).

The final issue addressed by Fried is Empowerment vs. Delivery of Services. In 1976 he asked a question that today still has not been addressed adequately by those involved with *human development*: "How can a society oriented to treating people by delivering professional services to them re-orient itself toward an empowering approach to human development?" (ibid., v). In answering this question, he distinguishes between the delivery of services and empowerment.

Fried states that the delivery of services means "implementing programs aimed at responding to the needs and problems of individuals" (ibid., 87). He argues that the problem with this approach is twofold. First, it causes the deliverers of services "to *evade*...responsibility to make...society more equitable, to share wealth and power more evenly" (ibid., 90). In other words, society tends to throw money at the problem and hopes that the problem will go away, and if it does not, then it creates more programs and packages to solve the problem. This evades responsibility at the local and individual level where problems can be addressed most adequately through education and empowerment.

Second, the delivery of services creates "an unreal dichotomy between the 'deliverers' and their 'targets'" (ibid.).   Since the professionals become so "expert" at what they do, they tend to make their clients feel like they do not know how to care for themselves (ibid., 90-91).   In Fried's experiment, the dichotomy was broken because people were learning skills that they could later integrate into their own lives.   In alignment with democratic principles of self-government, an enlightened electorate enlightened.

The alternative approach to delivery of services is empowerment.   Fried defines empowerment as assisting people to "gain the strength and gather the resources to begin to bring about what they feel to be the good life in society" (ibid., 93-94).   To do this, he suggests that communities create settings in which its members can exercise power that does not exploit other members, involve participants in cultural programs at all levels of decision-making, assist them to gain a sense of ownership in these programs, encourage members to share roles as both teacher and learner, and inspire people by making them have a sense of self-worth and to be self-critical and reflective about their own actions (ibid., 94).

The hoped for outcome of individual empowerment is that it will lead toward an "empowered society."   Fried describes this as a society "in which human beings view themselves not as 'deliverers,' exclusively, nor only as 'recipients' of human services, but as one class of responsibly interdependent people, *all* of whom have needs and problems, *all* of whom have skills and sensitivities and not-yet-developed potential, *all* of whom serve others as they themselves are served" (ibid.).

But creating an empowered society cannot occur solely through those seeking to be empowered. The State also has an important role in fostering the conditions for empowerment. In order to allow empowerment to happen, the role of government "should be to outlaw obstacles to human welfare and to break up those institutional monopolies which force us to consume bureaucratic packages of services" (ibid., 92).

The CLC Project

The CLC Project was an attempt by Fried to explore the idea of "learning-in-community" and the four aforementioned philosophical issues. As previously stated, he worked with eight small communities in New Hampshire to create Community Learning Centers through a "core group" of people within each community.

Fried defines a CLC as a core group of people in a community who brings "informal programs of life-long learning to small towns and neighborhoods which might not otherwise be able to offer community learning programs to their citizens" (1980, 5). The "Core Group" (CG) is that group of people, approximately eight to fourteen people, who serves as "the basis of CLC organization in each participating community." They are themselves "potential learners and instructors" who decide "what the CLC is to be within their town: what name to give the project, who will organize what learning activities, where they will take place, and so forth" (ibid.). In a real sense the "Core Group IS the CLC" (ibid.).

The learning activities that the CG organizes are all informal, non-credit, tuition-free, community-based, adult education programs that could range from quilt-

making to ski lessons (ibid., 5).   The factors that influence the development of a
learning program by a CG include (ibid.):

- How long the members have been working together and how much experience they
  have gained?

- What kinds of people comprise the group?

- Who in the group or in the community can be identified as local resource persons?

- What kinds of requests are being received by the CG from the community?

- What kinds of activities can be offered by the CG to the greater community?

In order to initiate the CLC Project, Fried took on the role of a
participant/facilitator that was financially supported by the State.   As a
participant/facilitator, his role was more of an organizer than a leader.   The primary
objective of the participant/facilitator is "always to *empower* citizens, within the
environment of the core group, to create and sustain an organization by providing
learning and self-help activities for the community" (ibid., 9).

Fried makes a clear distinction between a leader, a manipulator, and a
facilitator.   A leader is one who "analyzes the problem, decides (perhaps after
conferring with advisors) what action to take, and then attempts to rally the community
or organization to support the leader's chosen course of action" (1980, 24).   A
manipulator "analyzes the problem to find solutions other people will accept and
especially which solution will work to his or her own advantage.   The manipulator
then attempts, often through covert or covertly coercive means, to influence others to

respond in ways that will best serve his/her ends" (ibid.).   A facilitator "attempts to bring people together to *collectively* analyze the problem, assists them in reviewing various options, supports them in coming to a decision either by consensus or by vote, and then helps them both to implement their decision and to reflect upon the whole process" (ibid.).   Though he makes the distinction between the three kinds of roles, he is careful to state that in practice these three roles are not mutually exclusive (ibid.).

Other aspects of the participant/facilitator include participating in discussions, reciprocity, empowerment, and liberation.   In cases where Fried wanted to take sides on a particular issue the core group was discussing, he acted as a participant and not as a facilitator.   He states, "As a *participant*, I could openly pursue the kind of atmosphere within a meeting that I enjoy participating in, i.e. flexible, informal, task-oriented, sociable, supportive of input from all present, open to new membership, and capable of reaching decisions through discussion and consensus" (1980, 28).

Reciprocity is another key aspect of the participant/facilitator.   Since service providers have been trained to take the problem-centered approach toward human services, it becomes very easy for them to establish "the perceived need of others as the basis for action" (ibid., 28).   Instead, the participant/facilitator should "relate to people in terms of reciprocity" (ibid.).   As Fried recalls in one meeting, a person said to him, "People don't like to be reminded about what they 'need'—not even by other people in town...These people have...a desire to learn" (ibid., 29).

Reciprocity is central to empowerment. Within the framework of "delivery of services," the emphasis is on a perceived need by the service provider. In the context of empowerment, need is removed and replaced with reciprocity toward those involved with the CLC. The participant/facilitator assists the members with becoming self-reliant learners and teachers by sharing his knowledge and skills (ibid., 29). Empowerment is "a *partnership*, a mutual sharing of ideas, intuitions, and experiences" between the professional and other people (ibid., 30).

Finally, Fried defines the role of participant/facilitator as one that is liberating in the sense that it frees the professional from "the charge that he or she is 'exploiting' those in need and perpetuating their dependency and inequality" (ibid., 30). The partnership between the professional and others implies that both parties understand the processes of human development: 1) working out of ignorance, 2) watching use of language, 3) facilitating conversation, 4) reinforcing people's expertise, 5) promoting active and passive ownership, and 6) modeling attitudes and behaviors (ibid., 30-32).

The participant/facilitator is a democratic role that one can take in assisting communities with developing a CLC. However, Fried notes some of the dilemmas of the participant/facilitator, such as inability to communicate one's agenda, a faction of the community could control the CG, difficult to build flexibility and accountability into the CG, difficult to learn if the project "message" is reaching the learners, and longevity of the CG is uncertain (ibid., 32-34).

Implementing the CLC Project

The aim of the CLC Project was "to develop both a *model* and a *process* through which groups of citizens...[Core Groups]...would acquire skills necessary to organize informal, non-credit, tuition-free learning activities, taught by volunteers from the community" (ibid., 5). In order to implement the project, Fried focused on small towns with populations of one thousand-five hundred to three thousand people. He contends that a benefit of smaller towns is that they "have enough informal, unorganized learning so that the CLC" could offer similar programs more than once, such as a quilt-making class taught several times a week by different people. In addition, the "different social classes and life-styles might be more likely to know each other and to interact comfortably, thus minimizing the all-too-real possibility of the CLC being captured by one social faction or another" (1980, 11).

Other reasons for the selection of small towns included reaffirming the value of the town members' community life by making it evident to them that an abundance of skilled people existed in their small towns, emphasizing the importance of self-sufficiency by making them identify their community resources, and encouraging them to run their own learning programs in order to emphasize the point that learning can happen on a small community level in informal ways (ibid.).

In addition to the above, Fried followed ten steps in creating and implementing the CLC Project in New Hampshire towns (ibid., 11-14).

1. Contacted people Fried knew in several organizations, such as the Jaycees, who might be privy to the idea of the project and introduce him to people in the towns who might want to serve as contact persons.

2. Contacted the possible "contact persons" and asked them if they would be willing to host a meeting for their town.

3. Worked with host (contact person) to select invitees in the community that were of friendly disposition, worked well with others, and represented several factions of the community.

4. Host contacted invitees and Fried followed up with a letter of invitation that was accompanied by information on the CLC Project.

5. Fried assisted host with preparations for meeting, such as video equipment.

6. When everyone arrived, Fried and the host welcomed the attendees and he gave a simple re-capitulation of the project.

7. The meeting began by Fried asking the person on his left questions such as, "Is there something about this idea that appeals to you?" or "Is there something you would particularly like to learn from somebody else in town?"

8. Fried would listen to each speaker and respond positively to his or her comments.

9. After the discussion, Fried would reaffirm what everyone had said and ask the group if they would be interested in moving ahead or scrapping the idea all together. At this point he explained about the CG.

10. If people agreed with participating in the CLC Project, normally four or five people would volunteer to form the nucleus of the CG and Fried would then meet with the CG for a while to set up the date, time, and location for the next meeting. Everyone else was invited to the next meeting even if they were not in the CG.   If

people knew of others who might be interested in the CLC Project, Fried asked them to invite those people to the next meeting.

The Core Group meetings were conducted in a participatory democratic fashion. The meetings were usually conducted in someone's house. Around 7:15 PM everyone would gather at the house. Between 7:15 PM and 8:00 PM informal discussion, along with coffee and cake, would take place until someone would say to start the meeting. The formal meeting usually consisted of an update on the activities that took place and followed with the setting of the evening's agenda. At the end of the meeting, around 10:00 PM, if a decision had to be made upon a particular issue, the decision was customarily made by consensus, and if consensus was not achieved, then the participants would think over the issue until the next meeting. The meetings always closed with a social time in which the participants could finish-up their earlier conversations with leftover coffee and cake. Finally, Fried made it his custom to encourage the group to act as a voluntary association by leaving the next meeting in charge of the group, and if people needed to get in contact with him, they could call him collect at the university (ibid., 16-19).

Conclusions

Fried drew five conclusions from his development, implementation, and participation in the CLC Project with small New Hampshire communities (1976, vi-vii).

1. Adult learners can develop and run their own programs without a large budget or outside funding.

2. "Empowerment" to learn and teach rests in the hands of the participants themselves, not some outside organization.

3. The Core Group model is the vehicle by which empowerment occurs.

4. The programs themselves become more complex as teacher/learners develop self-confidence in designing and implementing programs.

5. Higher education can be a partner with community learning only if it "adapts itself to the citizenry" and not the other way around.

In comparing the CLC Project with other educational service programs across the state, Fried gained some important insights. First, the CLC Project was most closely aligned to programs that were independent, informal, and voluntary. Second, it was least similar to programs that referred to themselves as "community education programs," "adult education programs," or "continuing education programs" since these programs were hierarchically organized. Third, it was relative to those organizations or groups that were connected with colleges or universities. Finally, the CLC Project's most unique feature was its emphasis on "Participant Ownership" and self-reliance where people through voluntary participatory democratic action came together to learn and provide learning in an open and free environment (ibid., Appendix A, 18-19).

Part 2
Research Approach

There is an increasing realization of the massive societal changes and transformations that are reflected in the new realities of the postindustrial information/knowledge era. These changes touch the lives of every person, family, community, and nation and define the future of humanity. However, we are entering the twenty-first century with organizations designed during the nineteenth century. Improvement or restructuring of existing systems, based on the design of the industrial machine age, does not work any more. Only a radical and fundamental change of perspective and purposes, and the redesign of our organizations and social systems, will satisfy the new realities and requirements of our era.

—Bela Banathy, 1996

Introduction

Bela Banathy's Systems Design Architecture is the research approach of this dissertation. It is a systems design approach that is presented in, *Designing Social Systems in a Changing World*, *Systems-View of Education*, and *Systems Design of Education*. Part 2 addresses the questions: "What is systems design?" "Why do we need it?" " When should we engage in design?" "Who should be the designers?" "What is the product of design?" and "How do we design?" In addition to answering these questions, Banathy's key ideas regarding systems design are addressed: image creation, design information, design solution, design experimentation and evaluation, and modeling.

Chapter 3: What is Design?

Design means many things to many different people, which includes architects, environmental designers, industrial designers, organizational designers, and social systems designers. For some, such as L. B. Archer, design is "the use of scientific principles, technical information, and imagination in the definition of a system to perform specific functions with maximum economy and efficiency" (quoted in Banathy 1996, 12). For others, like Banathy, design is "a future-creating, collective human activity" that empowers people "to exercise truly participative democracy" (1996, 1-2).

Design takes place within the realm of social systems design. A social system is defined here as *a meaningful system that is intentionally and collectively designed by a community of self-actualizing individuals for the guidance of human evolutionary development and the direction of positive social development*. A community, by Walter Nicgorski's definition, is "rooted in the individual and is formed, led and enriched by distinct responsible persons. Rather than a collectivity of people, it is a mutual sharing of their particular endowments" (1986, 326). Thus, a working definition of social systems design can be extrapolated for the development of an alternative learning framework for community learning centers.

A Working Definition of Design

> *Systems design is a community of self-actualizing individuals, that is, a group of people who mutually share their values, interests, ideals, and knowledge that is germane to the system to be created, and who, through participatory democratic actions, creatively design meaningful systems that are shared with the greater community toward the guidance of human evolutionary development and the direction of positive social development.*

Design has an Intellectual Culture

Design has an intellectual culture. Banathy declares that in order for a culture to be recognized as a distinct culture it must have its own "knowledge and understanding; ways of knowing, thinking, and doing; beliefs and dispositions; and customs and habits, shared by people, and passed on through social transmission" (ibid., 33).

The intellectual culture of design differs from the intellectual cultures of the sciences and the humanities. The culture of the sciences concerns itself with truth— the study of the natural world as it is. The culture of the humanities deals with human emotion—the exploration and portrayal of the human experience. The culture of design pertains to future making—the creation of social systems that do not exist yet (ibid.). Table 1 illustrates the differences between the three cultures.

Table 1. The Three Cultures (Banathy 1996, 34)

	Science	Humanities	Design
Focus	The Natural World	The Human Experience	The Man-made World
	Problem Finding	Understand the Human Experience	Solution Finding
	Describe "What Is"	Portray It	What "Should Be"
Primary Methods	Experimentation	Analogy	Modeling
	Pattern Recognition	Metaphor	Pattern Formation
	Analysis	Criticism	Synthesis
	Classification	Valuation	Conjecture
	Deduction	Induction	Abduction
What is Valued	Objectivity	Subjectivity	Practicality
	Rationality	Imagination	Creativity
	Neutrality	Commitment	Empathy
	Concern for "Truth"	Concern for "Justice"	Concern for "Goodness of Fit"

Design is a Mode of Inquiry

In addition to differences with science and the humanities, design has similarities and differences with the other modes of inquiry: planning, problem solving, improvement, and restructuring. Furthermore, design is systemic design inquiry, not systematic design inquiry. Systematic design is the design of social systems via a logical and sequential process (Banathy 1996, 16). On the other hand, systemic design is a "creative, disciplined, and decision-oriented inquiry, carried out in iterative cycles" that has three characteristics. These characteristics are the specialized techniques to approach the problem-situation, generative rules for the techniques, and universal principles of design that guide in designing the new system (ibid.).

Shared Characteristics of Planning and Design

The characteristics that planning and design share include disciplined thinking, rational behavior, or logical processes; a set of purposeful activities that follow some form of methodology to reach the goals (Banathy 1996, 18). Furthermore, the new knowledge and information that is part of planning or design is collected, categorized, and evaluated so that choices can be made and then synthesized into a comprehensive plan or design (ibid.).

Differences between Planning and Design

The first difference between planning and design has to do with complexity. Design entails far more complexity than does planning. Design is a "sequence of tasks organized in a time and resources frame;" whereas planning is a "set of steps that one takes toward a goal" (ibid.). Design is a "description of a system that has the capacity/capability to attain set purposes" and planning is the means to "bring the design to life" (ibid.).

A second difference between planning and design concerns the approaches toward problem situations. Design takes a *holistic* approach toward understanding problem situations in that it seeks to understand them "as a system of interconnected, interdependent, and interacting problems and creates the design solution as a system of interconnected, interdependent, interacting, and internally consistent solution ideas" (ibid., 19). However, planning involves solving problems by an "incremental, piece-meal, disjointed, and part-oriented approach" with the hope that the greater issue of the problem situation will be resolved (ibid. 18-19).

Differences between Problem Solving and Design

The first difference between problem solving and design is focus. Problem solving focuses on finding or selecting the problem to solve, analyzing and structuring the problem, selecting the methods to address the problem, resolving the problem, and presenting and evaluating the solution (ibid., 19). However, systems design as a disciplined inquiry focuses on creating an image of the desired system, selecting design approaches and methods to create a design solution and alternatives, and describing or modeling the most appropriate design solution (ibid.).

Another difference between problem solving and design is the circumstances within which they are employed. The problem solving approach works best when the problem is well-defined and well-structured; whereas the systems design approach is most applicable when one is unable to stay within the bounds of the problem and must focus on the solution and not the problem (ibid., 20).   As Banathy phrases it, "If solutions could be offered within the existing system, there would be no need to design. Thus, designers have to transcend the existing system…create a different system or devise a new one" (ibid.).

Differences between Improvement and Design

Improvement focuses on making what exists now more effective and efficient by examining the specific parts of the system (ibid., 20).   Design focuses on getting what is required from the entire system, not from its particular parts.   This requires viewing the system from a holistic perspective, determining the interrelationships between the parts and how they function as a whole (ibid., 20-21).

Differences between Restructuring and Design

Restructuring is concerned with reorganizing a structure of a system by rearranging the parts differently to create a new configuration using the same parts (ibid., 21).   Restructuring attempts to correct what is wrong with the current system by rearranging the functions and components of the system (ibid.).   However, design is concerned with creating a new image of the existing system, defining the purposes of the new system based upon the image, and designating the functions that are necessary for achieving the purpose of the new system.   Once the system is designed and purposes and functions are well defined, designers later become concerned with the restructuring of the components.   The "iron law" of design is "form follows function" (ibid.).

Design is Decision-Oriented

Another important aspect of systems design is the kinds of systems designs that are possible. Two types of systems design are currently employed: conclusion-oriented disciplined inquiry and decision-oriented disciplined inquiry. Conclusion-oriented disciplined inquiry is formally used within the natural and behavioral sciences to describe the nature of things and how they work (Banathy 1996, 22). Thus, when researchers and scholars study systems design as a subject of inquiry they will employ conclusion-oriented disciplined inquiry because they are drawing upon the general knowledge of design and the findings of other disciplines and fields of inquiry that are germane to the subject and context of design (ibid., 24-25).

On the other hand, decision-oriented disciplined inquiry is used by the professions and different social service fields for designing social systems that will achieve a future that they believe should be (ibid., 23-24). The focus is on design and outcomes, not descriptions and findings—the "salient intellectual process" of design is synthesis that is accompanied by an expansionist orientation which works to formulate and fulfill a purpose (ibid., 22). Figure 1 illustrates the relationship between the two domains of disciplined inquiry.

Figure 1. Banathy's Map of Disciplined Inquiry (ibid., 24)

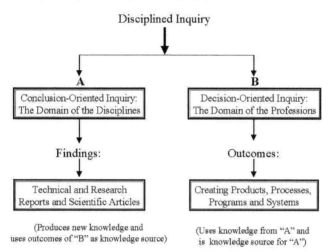

For systems design to be considered a discipline of inquiry, it must satisfy three conditions:

- **Design must be located within the larger inquiry space of disciplined inquiry** (ibid., 23). Designers will first and foremost create images of a new future system, develop alternative images, evaluate the alternatives, and categorize the alternatives to best and least qualified, and finally choose the most qualified alternative for the desired system (ibid., 24).

- **Design must have its relationships with other types of disciplined inquiries explored** (ibid., 23). These include the representing, describing, characterizing, and modeling systems and processes; analyzing, diagnosing, assessing, and evaluating such systems and processes; planning, adjusting, and improving the system and its processes; developing, implementing, and institutionalizing systems and processes; and finally, managing the system (ibid., 25).

- **Design must have its domains identified** (ibid., 23).   The domain within which the design of an alternative framework for CLCs operates is the human activity systems.   Other domains include abstract, conceptual systems (theories); physical systems (buildings); hybrid, machine-nature systems (plasma waste converter); and man-machine systems (automobiles) (ibid., 25-26).

Chapter 4: Why Do We Need Systems Design?

Design is needed to deal with the complexities of the everyday world and to give people a greater stake in the systems that are created for them. The two underlying purposes of design include:

1. Ability to Deal with Complexity and Chaos

   The educational system, media, and culture have conditioned people to avoid dealing with complexity. People prefer to know the problem, why it exists, and find the answers rather than face the reality that problems are much more inter-related, difficult to assess, and sometimes impossible to answer precisely.

2. Ability to Understand and Participate in the Design of Social Systems

   People can remain ignorant of systems design and continue to fall victim to the systems that are created for them; or they can become literate in systems design and democratically participate in the design of their social systems that will lead them toward a more humane and just world.

Dealing with Problems

The first purpose of systems design deals with problems or problem situations. Banathy identifies two aspects and four categories of problems. The two aspects are structured problems and unstructured problems (1996, 27). Structured problems are "explicitly stated and imply that a theory concerning their solution is available" and are dealt with by systems engineers and operations research (ibid.). However, unstructured problems are "manifested with a feeling of unease, and they cannot be explicitly stated without oversimplifying them" and are dealt with by systems designers.

The four categories of problems include simple, compound, complex, and metaproblems. Simple problems are "understood in terms of a specified number of calculable variables and are subject to analysis and optimization" (ibid., 27). Compound problems are "defined in terms of an unspecified number of variables that are calculable" (ibid.). Complex problems are "definable in terms of a specified number of incalculable variables and are approached by exploring all variables and initiating systemic change in the overall situation" (ibid.). Metaproblems are the most difficult to solve because they are "made up of an unknown number of variables and are addressed by exploring those that are most relevant to contemplating [a] solution to the problem situation" (ibid., 27-28).

Systems design addresses complex and metaproblems since it entails envisioning a future that does not exist and employing methods that have not been defined. When complex or metaproblems in systems design are considered, it is important to think of these problems as unbounded problems, that is, problem situations which "compose a system of problems rather than a collection of problems" (ibid. 29). One of the pitfalls of addressing problem situations is the assumption that all problems come nicely wrapped accompanied by a toolkit of methods to solve them. The nature of systems design is working with social systems that are unbounded, dynamic, and continuously interactive, and this means that the problem situations will also be unbounded, dynamic and continuously interactive (ibid., 28-31). Therefore, Banathy contends that it must be recognized that "there is no logical way of determining the right level at which to state and tackle a design problem" (ibid., 30).

Furthermore, when determining how to address a problem, the aspects of the problem, such as substantive, locus, and value need to be considered. The substantive aspect considers using the most appropriate methodology (ibid. 28). For example, in designing a new learning framework for community learning centers, a decision-oriented approach is employed instead of a conclusion-oriented approach because the purpose is to create a future that SHOULD BE. The locus of a problem focuses on the situation as a whole and solutions to the specific needs and resources are created (ibid.). For example, a transformational learning framework for CLCs assists a community with designing its learning system in accordance with its particular environment and situation. The value aspect of a problem is framed within the context of the members' aspirations (ibid.). When designing its own learning network, a community will design it in accordance with the hopes and aspirations that the community has for itself, not in accordance with a standardized approach to design and development.

Literacy, Competency, and Interactiveness

The second purpose of systems design is for people to understand and participate in the design of social systems so they do not become victims of despotism. This is in alignment with Thomas Jefferson's vision of an enlightened electorate:

> I know no safe depository of the ultimate powers of the society but the people themselves; and if we think them not enlightened enough to exercise their control with wholesome discretion, the remedy is not to take it from them, but to inform their discretion by education. (In a letter to William Charles Jarvis, September 28, 1820, and quoted in Appleby and Ball, 1999, 382)

When Banathy discusses design literacy, he means that an educated citizenry should understand that design is a human activity with certain operations which work according to certain systemic design principles. Second, the citizenry should be attentive to the fact that design has an important role in a democratic society as well as the role that each person plays in design. Third, it should be aware of the implications that design has upon the greater society, such as the quality of life and human development (Banathy 1996, 36). Finally, an educated citizenry should create opportunities for itself to participate in design so it can gain competency in the skill (ibid.). This in turn will create a "design culture" that enables them to create a participatory democratic environment (ibid., 36-37).

Chapter 5: When Should We Engage in Design?   Who Should Design?

<u>When?</u>

Banathy states that in system dynamics there are two kinds of feedback loops: negative and positive.   Negative feedback signals that things need to be corrected in the system in order to attain its stated outcomes (Banathy 1996, 54).   It works best when the system environment is stable and requires only few piecemeal approaches. Positive feedback, on the other hand, is used when designing a new system.   It signals that the system needs to self-create and co-evolve with the greater environment (ibid.).

Design should be undertaken when new realities emerge that stand in opposition to the current social system and when the beliefs and values of the community are no longer commensurate with the system.   This is especially so for educational systems in the United States.   Educators now recognize that education should be person-centered and assist people toward their self-actualization.   However, current educational systems in the United States were not designed for this purpose. They were designed to meet the needs of a growing nineteenth and twentieth century industrial economy that was allowing more European immigrants into America.   The emphasis was on "Americanizing" them in the most effective and efficient way possible, that is, providing them with the skills necessary to live effectively as American citizens. However, a nineteenth and twentieth century industrial economy no longer exists in America.   Furthermore, new realities about human growth and development have emerged, as well as a change in beliefs and values about education.   In this situation, new educational systems should be designed in order for them to be commensurate with the realities and belief and value systems of the new society.

<u>Who?</u>

In 1900 Dewey believed that workers should have a voice in the industrial system that they were helping to create and not be "mere appendages to the machines they operate!" Banathy makes a similar point when he describes design as a "democratically participative activity." When creating a social system, all those effected by the system should have a stake in its design (1996, 50). Only through democratic participation can democratic principles be actualized and add value to the society as a whole. This is what Jefferson meant by an "enlightened electorate." The kinds of persons involved in design should be those who demonstrate the following salient attributes (ibid., 54):

1. Confidence and Courage—the ability to shift from one paradigm to another requires the designer to enter the unknown.

2. Situational Sensitivity—the ability to perceive things that others may not.

3. Flexibility—the ability to adjust quickly to new and emerging developments in the design environment.

4. Tolerance—the ability to deal calmly with ambiguity and uncertainty as one tries to understand the meaning of contradictions and dynamic complexities.

5. Interactive Movement—the ability to move between analysis and synthesis interactively.

6. Management—the ability to guide the design using situation-specific design methods while also seeking design-solutions for the new processes of the system.

Chapter 6: What is the Product of Design?

The product of design is a model of the system. The process of developing a model is called "model building" (Banathy 1996, 50). Model building assists designers in creating and testing several alternative solutions of a future system rather than designing and implementing a whole system that they think might work and then realize later that it does not (ibid., 51).

The term model can have several meanings, but Banathy refers to the basic notion that underlies all the different meanings—"a construct or description that represents or stands for something" (ibid.). The two classifications of models that are worked with in systems design are product and process models. Product models describe inquiry outcomes; whereas, process models describe the processes and activities by which the inquiry is conducted (ibid.). Product models are ontological because they answer the questions, "What is?" or "What should be?" Process models are epistemological because they address the methods that are used in designing the model.

In addition to the two classifications of a model, the three characteristics of a model include: 1) a clear description of a future system, 2) a facilitation of communication between all groups that are participating in the design, and 3) guidance so people are empowered to implement the design according to their own circumstances (ibid., 52).

Chapter 7: How Do We Design Social Systems?

Social systems are designed according to a systemic approach and designers focus on discovering solutions.   A rigid structure of design as analysis—synthesis—evaluation is unrealistic because social systems are too complex to be neatly "boxed." In fact, analysis, synthesis, and evaluation operate ubiquitously in complex systems and require the designer to choose approaches that create a model that meets the design criteria (Banathy 1996, 56).   This is why designers early on in the design process develop a set of core ideas that tell what the system should be, which Banathy refers to as the First Image of the System.   Figure 2 illustrates the synergistic relationship of analysis, synthesis, and evaluation in the development of the First Image of the System.

Figure 2. Synergy in Creating the First Image of the System

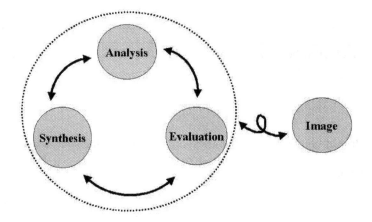

Several models have been developed that incorporate a synergistic relationship of analysis, synthesis, and evaluation, but most of these have been developed for the corporate or business community (ibid., 57-61). However, Banathy's Social Systems Design which was used to create his "Learning Society," is more appropriate for those involved in educational systems since it addresses transcending, envisioning, designing, presenting/displaying, and finally planning in terms of educational matters.

Transcending the Current Paradigm

Transcending the current system to a desired future system requires designers to express the vision, ideas, and aspirations of the desired future. It can be expressed as, "We should live in a world that ~." Transcending is an exploration into the unknown and requires designers to understand the current system.

In order to navigate from the current state toward a desired future state, Banathy suggests that designers use an Option Field, a framework that establishes design inquiry boundaries and creates design options of a desired future system (ibid., 63). An option field consists of four dimensions: focus of inquiry, scope, relationships with other systems, and types of systems. Within each dimension there are a multitude of possible options that work from a closed system to an open system (ibid.). Figure 3 illustrates an option field that could be used for the design of a community learning center system.

Figure 3.   Option Field for a CLC System

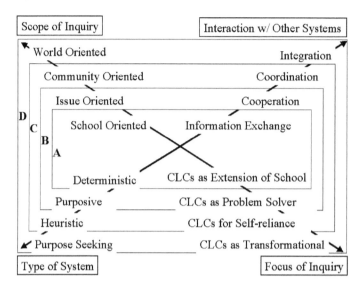

The Focus of Inquiry allows designers to conceptualize the system at four different levels.   At the most rigid level, CLCs are viewed as an extension of the school system by offering after-school activities, such as with the U.S. 21st Century CLC Program.   At the next level, CLCs are seen as problem solvers by offering services in adult literacy programs or computer literacy programs to the greater community, such as with the USAID LearnLink Program.   At a greater level, CLCs are places that build self-reliance.   This would be similar to the New York City CUE CLC Program in which parents empowered themselves to rely more upon their own abilities and their own democratic participation in the educational system than upon the system itself. Finally, CLCs are seen as transformational, such as with the Jewish Community Centers of Chicago.   A transformational CLC is one that strives to assist with individual transformation (*paideia*), community transformation (developing and maintaining, through participatory democratic actions, community sustainability and self-reliance), and spiritual transformation (the ability to move from beneficial life to contributive life) (ibid., 64).   The question that each community should ask itself in choosing how to construct CLCs is, "At which level to focus on CLCs?"

The Scope of Inquiry for the option field in this paper includes school oriented, issue oriented, community oriented, and world oriented.   If the scope of inquiry is field (A) school oriented and field (B) issue oriented, then design is not possible because at these levels focus is still within the context of the current school system.   Only by entering into field (C) do the boundaries extend into the community and interact with other systems.   The designers contemplate the synergy between CLCs and other systems.   If the focus is in field (D), then all the issues that have affected or will continue to affect education globally are explored, such as the characteristics of the postindustrial or knowledge/information society and huge changes and transformations in the cultural, economic, technical, scientific, and organizational spheres of societies (ibid., 65).   Furthermore, this exploration assists in considering the implications that these events have for education: redefining the purposes and functions of education, developing new methods and applications to attain these purposes, and creating new organizational environments that are conducive to the new methods and applications for learning and human development (ibid.).

The Relationship with Other Systems dimension explores how CLCs can interact with other systems.   CLCs can be involved in information exchange, such as exchanging information on teaching methods.   They can participate in cooperation, such as two history teachers from two different schools working together on a history

103

project with their classes at a CLC. They can join in coordination, such as CLCs working together with museums in providing educational opportunities for children. They can also play a part in integration, such as creating CLCs that will co-evolve with other systems so as to assist with the overall learning process and spur human development (ibid., 65).

Because CLCs are entities within an educational system, they can be of four different system types: deterministic, purposive, heuristic, and purpose seeking (ibid., 65). Deterministic systems are unitary closed systems that have clearly defined goals which limit people's degree of freedom to select methods or applications for working within the system. The activities within the system are mechanistic. Examples of a deterministic system include industrial and government bureaucracies and centralized national educational systems (ibid., 65).

Purposive systems are also unitary systems. Their goals are established from the top down; however, they are more open than deterministic systems and react to change more quickly. People are given more freedom to choose methods and applications for teaching or working within the system. Purposive systems are most readily found in corporations, social service agencies, and decentralized educational systems (ibid., 65-66).

Heuristic and purpose-seeking systems concern systems designers. Heuristic systems are pluralistic, dynamic, and systemic. Because of their nature, they are able to develop broad policy guidelines and goals in order to initiate policy. Furthermore,

104

they react to change faster than purposive systems and have the additional ability of initiating change. Heuristic systems can be found in today's most advanced research and development institutions (ibid., 66).

Purpose-seeking systems are similar to heuristic systems in that they are dynamic, systemic, and pluralistic. However, unlike heuristic systems, they seek to actualize the ideal future and co-evolve with other systems in their environment. Purpose-seeking systems are best found in communities that integrate their educational, social services, and human development systems (ibid., 66).

The option framework has great implications for design because designers can consider various aspects of the model. First, they can ask, "Why should a particular option be chosen?" In addressing this question, they explore the values, assumptions, preferences, and ideas that serve as the foundation for the system to be created. Second, the option field addresses whether or not there is consistency between the choice and the future that is to be constructed and if this choice is compatible with the values, assumptions, preferences, and ideas that are believed to be true (ibid., 66).

Envisioning the Image of the New System

The next step in designing a new system is to create an image of that system. Imaging is grounded in the values, assumptions, and ideals of the system designers. Banathy quotes O. W. Markley and Willis Harman who assert that an image underlies the "ways in which the society shapes its institutions, educates its young, and goes about whatever it perceives its business to be" (1996, 68). Furthermore, Kenneth

Boulding contends that images are based upon three propositions: 1) values are directly linked to the image to be created, 2) behavior in the system is dependent upon the image that is created, and 3) the experiences within the system serve as messages for either adjusting the image or altering it altogether (ibid., 69).   He also pronounces that most images can be found in the "perennial philosophy," that is to say, images can be "found in the traditional lore of cultures as well as in advanced philosophy and in the ancient and contemporary forms of religion" (ibid.).

The *International Community Learning Center Network's* values and image of a community learning center system in Table 2 illustrate a set of values and an image for a CLC system.

Table 2. Values and Image of a CLC System (ICLC Network, 2000)

Values	Image
1. Every person has inclinations toward certain types of human activity and that the individual must be allowed to discover these inclinations. 2. The human race as a whole is in a process of evolutionary consciousness that transcends both mind and spirit. Thus, the primary activity of our species should be education. 3. In order to foster this evolution, our social structures should assist individuals with developing their innate abilities and to help them reach their vocational and avocational goals that are appropriate to their particular abilities. 4. Work[1] allows a person to fulfill his or her actualization, and that no person should do work that is incommensurate with his or her being. 5. An individual should only be entitled to those things that assist with his or her actualization, and that claiming things that are incommensurate with an individual's self deprives others of their actualization[2]. 6. The best kind of government is government that is closest to the people. 7. The market[3] exists for the benefit of the people so they may acquire those goods and services for sustaining life and living out integral lives. -- 1. Work here does not refer to the modern capitalistic notion of an activity performed in exchange for economic benefit. 2. This means that if you as an individual know who you are, then you will only make claim to those things that assist with your actualization. In this situation, no one is deciding for you, you are deciding for yourself what things you need or do not need. 3. The market here is defined by Alvin Toffler as "nothing more than an exchange network, a switchboard, as it were, through which goods or services, like messages, are routed to their appropriate destinations." It does not refer to the capitalistic notion of the market.	1. A CLC should serve as a nerve center for the universal learning network and provide for the people of its community individualized learning programs in order to give all people of all ages access to any learning resource at any time (Moffett, 1994). 2. A CLC should be a learning ecology and a laboratory for learning. 3. A CLC should be developed using organic architectural principles, principles that are concerned with "the building, the community the building is set in, and the architect, builder, and patron's vision about the facility" (Conrad, 1976), for example, developing CLCs within walking distance to people's homes. It would also include searching for techniques that create a self-sustaining facility that employ renewable resources and allow the facility structure itself to help with learning about systems, holism, and the fragility and wonder of life, the earth, and the universe. 4. A CLC should employ principles of consensus democracy (administration and governance). 5. A CLC should allow its members to design, create and participate in the learning community; and support community research and development in order to help better facilitate learning and communication throughout the universal learning network, such as research and development of electronic learning devices. 6. A CLC should support the on-going learning, action-research and development to empower professional and non-professional educators (network guides, learning facilitators), resource coordinators, and learning center core staff—and the whole community—to participate in the creation of healthy and sustainable communities.

Designing the System

       Designing the system involves conceptualizing and testing potential solution alternatives and selecting the most desirable one (Banathy 1996, 71). Banathy's Design Architecture is a mental model or process that one goes through to create the most desirable outcome of the design inquiry. It consists of five spaces that are interactive, co-evolutionary, and synergistic. These spaces include: 1) exploration and image creation space, 2) design information and knowledge space, 3) design solution space, 4) evaluation and experimentation space, and 5) modeling space. Figure 4 illustrates Banathy's Design Architecture.

Figure 4. Banathy's Design Architecture (ibid., 72)

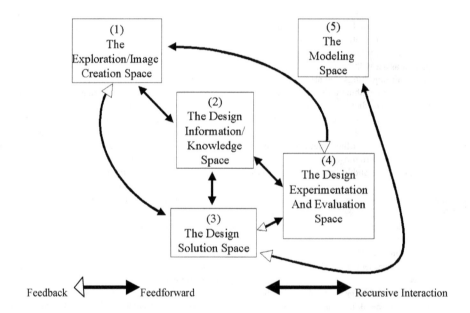

The exploration and image space includes all the previous activities: establishing inquiry boundaries (scope of inquiry, interaction with other systems, type of system, and focus of inquiry), exploring and choosing design options, generating a list of core values, and finally creating the image (ibid., 72).

The design information and knowledge space is reserved for that knowledge which was created through the recursive exploration and image creation space. It includes: 1) design content and context, 2) system environmental characteristics, and 3) design models, methods, and tools (ibid.).

In the design solution space a core definition of the social system is created, the system's specifications are listed, the functions of the system are explained, and the enabling systems that implement the functions identified, such as the management system and the organization and systemic environment (ibid., 73-74).

The evaluation and experimentation space is used for experimenting with solution alternatives and evaluating them using evaluation criteria that are in alignment with the image, the core definition, and specifications (ibid.). After deciding upon the best solution alternative, it is placed within the modeling space. It is within this space that the actual representation of the system and its systemic environment that were designed are presented (ibid.).

The dynamics of the spaces are illustrated in Figures 5 and 6. Figure 5 contains five spirals that illustrate the process of developing the model. Figure 6 illustrates the divergent and convergent nature of design. When developing the option field, the current paradigm is diverged, stretching the framework as far as it will go. Once options are chosen, an image of the future system is created and the model of the future system is converged (ibid., 73-75).

Figure 5. The Dynamics of Banathy's Design Architecture (Banathy 1996, 74)

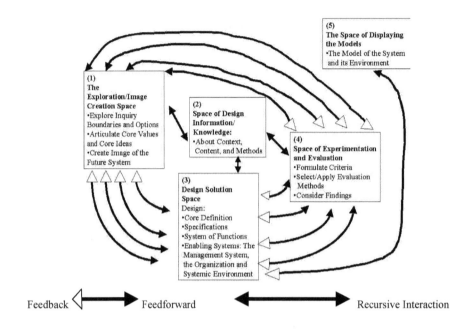

Figure 6. The Dynamics of Divergence and Convergence in Design Architecture (ibid., 75)

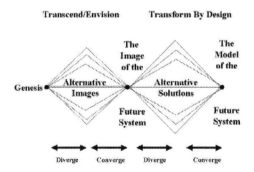

The first spiral, "Mission Statement and Purposes," is the formulation of a core definition or mission statement of the future system.   In Table 3, the mission statement addresses what the system will do for learners and the community, the environment, other systems, its members, and itself (Banathy 1991, 178).

Table 3.   Examples of Mission Statements

Elements of System	**Option 1** CLCs as Extension of School	**Option 2** CLCs as Problem Solvers	**Option 3** CLCs for Self Reliance	**Option 4** CLCs as Transformational
Learners and Community	Provides its students with after-school activities in a drug-free environment.	Assists adults with developing basic literacy skills.	Provides programs in leadership development that empowers parents to take a more active role in school affairs.	Provide for learners learning resources and arrangements that assist them in actualizing their true potentials.
Environment	Closed	Design, develop, and offer programs and arrangements that create an enlightened electorate so all can contribute to the greater democratic community.	Design, develop, and offer programs and arrangements that encourage parents to not only become more involved in school affairs but with all aspects of democratic institutions within the community.	Encourage the creation of a true learning society in which all individuals are able to contribute to one another's learning despite geographical differences.
Other Systems	Closed	Assist other government agencies with achieving adult literacy goals.	Assist schools with understanding better the concerns of parents and their children.	Integrate functions with other learning organizations or human services, such as museums.
Its Members	Develop a learning community that focuses on achieving the "basics" of education.	Develop a learning community that encourages adults to continue their own literacy education.	Develop a learning community in which parents, teachers, and administrators are working in concert for the greater good of the school.	Develop a learning community in which all are able to participate and contribute to the greater good of learning and becoming human.
Itself	Become a system that works cooperatively with teachers and others within the school.	Become a system that works cooperatively with adults and other social agencies in achieving adult literacy goals.	Become a system that works cooperatively with parents, teachers, and administrators in order to meet district-wide educational goals.	Become a transformational system in which individuals are transforming themselves daily, from the mental to the spiritual.

Purposes are a direct reflection of the image that is to be created. Purposes for a transformational CLC system could be similar to the list below:

- Serve as a nerve center for the universal learning network and provide for the people of its community individualized learning programs in order to give all people of all ages access to any learning resource at any time.

- Be a learning ecology and a laboratory for learning.

- Be developed using organic architectural principles.

- Employ principles of consensus democracy (administration and governance).

- Allow its members to design, create and participate in the learning community; and support community research and development in order to help better facilitate learning and communication throughout the universal learning network, such as research and development of electronic learning devices.

- Support the on-going learning, action-research and development to empower professional and non-professional educators (network guides, learning facilitators), resource coordinators, and learning center core staff—and the whole community— to participate in the creation of healthy and sustainable communities.

In spiral two, "Specifications," several questions are addressed (Banathy 1996, 76), such as, "Who are the clients of the system?" and "What services should the system offer?" In order to answer these questions, designers need to refer to the design solution space that includes the image, mission statement, and purposes. The answers are then assessed in the exploration space. This occurs by comparing the answers to the criteria with the image, mission statement, and purposes. If some of the answers are not commensurate with the criteria, then the designers spiral back to the exploration/image-creation space and re-formulate the design ideas and image of the future system. If the answers are commensurate with the image, it is necessary to spiral back to the design solution space to develop the system of functions (ibid.).

Spiral three, "System's Functions," sets boundaries for the future system. Boundaries in the option field are not the same as boundaries for the future system. Boundaries for the option field were established in order to choose the best alternative system to develop. Since a system has now been decided upon, the next task is to create the boundaries for the future system (Banathy 1991, 182). Important questions to ask include (Banathy 1996, 76), "What are the key functions that have to be carried out that enable the system to attain its mission and meet its specifications?" or "How do these functions interact to constitute a system of functions?"

To address these questions, a system of functions is designed (Banathy 1991, 183). The model represents a system that does not exist yet but is in the process of being designed (ibid., 184). The functions are developed that give rise to the form of the system that cannot be seen. Furthermore, function is about action, and action verbs are used to state what it is the system and subsystems will do (ibid.). To determine if the answers are commensurate with the image, mission statement, purposes, and newly created specifications, the answers are evaluated based upon the same set of criteria for the "Specifications" established earlier (Banathy 1991, 185).

The fourth spiral, "Enabling Systems," consists of three subspirals: management system, organization system, and the systemic environment (Banathy 1996, 76).   The management system is designed to ensure that the implementation of system functions will occur as it is explained in the Functions Model.   Designers ask (Banathy 1991, 189), "Was a plan conceived to initiate action that provides appropriate response to carrying out the functions and guide the action taken?" or "Were individual and collective performances motivated and energized?"

The organizational system subspiral explores how the organizational capacity and staff capability will be created to carry out functions in the Functions Model.   This exploration takes place by asking questions such as (ibid.), "What organizational and personal capabilities are required to carry out the identified functions?" or "What system components and people will have those capacities and capabilities?"

The "Systemic Environment" is the synthesis of all the spirals into a comprehensive system that adequately describes the future system.   It is presented in the "displaying the model space" that consists of three relationships—systems-environment model, functions/structure model, and the process/behavioral model (Banathy 1996, 77).   Table 4 presents these three models.

Table 4. Three Systems Models that Portray Design Outcomes (Banathy 1991, 79-80)

Systems-Environment Model **(Birds-Eye View)**	Observes the relational arrangements and dynamics between the learning system and its environment (global, national, regional, and local environments).
Functions/Structure Model **(Snap-Shot View)**	Observes the system at a given moment in time in order to see what the system is and what it does.
Process/Behavioral Model **(Motion Picture View)**	Observes the behavior of the system throughout time.

Presenting/Displaying the Future System

The "Displaying the Model Space" presents the model of the new system. The systems-environment model is a "birds-eye" view of the learning system. It portrays the relational arrangements between the system components and dynamics between the system and its environment (ibid., 79). The model provides a detailed description of the environment and system boundaries, definitions of the input and output entities that enter and exit the social system, definitions of the relationships and interactions between the system and environment, and a description of those processes that differentiate between those adjustments for improving the system or those changes for re-designing the whole system (ibid., 79-80).

The functions/structure model is a "snap shot" picture of the learning system that portrays it at a given moment in time (ibid., 79). All the components are developed and synthesized into a structured system: the image, mission statement, statement of purposes, specifications that characterize the system, system functions, and enabling systems (ibid., 80).

The process/behavioral model is a "motion picture" view of the learning system. It shows what the model does throughout the course of time (ibid., 79). It describes how the system processes input, that is, how it identifies, receives, screens, and assesses input into the social system and how it categorizes that input so it may be sent onto the transformation process to be transformed into the desired output. The model describes how transformation takes place in terms of production, facilitation, and guidance. A third aspect of the process/behavioral model is the processing of output. Similar to the transformation process, the process/behavioral model describes how output is produced, facilitated, and guided. Finally, the model describes how the product before becoming output is assessed and how the system analyzes and interprets evidence gathered for such an assessment (ibid., 81).

Planning the Future System

Planning how to implement the design of the future learning system is the final phase before actual implementation. The flexible plan is important because it will serve as a guide in determining how the design will be implemented. Systems Design Architecture is an on-going process that calls for flexibility and ingenuity to meet new and unexpected situations or demands. There are three important aspects of planning: defining and displaying the design, contemplating the implications the design might have once implemented, and finally a description or definition of the design implementation functions (Banathy 1996, 84).

Part 3
Creating the Image

Fools act on imagination without knowledge, pedants act on knowledge without imagination.

— *Alfred North Whitehead*

Introduction

The above quote by Alfred North Whitehead should serve as a warning to people as they go about designing their social systems. Designers cannot act upon imagination alone without an adequate understanding of the realities of their world, and likewise, they cannot create new knowledge without some form of creativity or ingenuity. Part 3, "Creating the Image," is a twofold process. First, it is the act of imagination that is supported by current realities and knowledge. Second, it is the creation of new knowledge for a future learning system.

In Part 2, two underlying purposes were identified for the use of systemic design architecture: 1) the ability to deal with complexity and chaos and 2) the ability to understand and participate in the design of social systems. Chapter 8 expands upon these contentions by exploring an alternative vision of society, new realities and their implications, and a vision of the future learning system that is to be created. It in effect is the construction of the knowledge base from which the image is to be made.

Chapter 9 is the actual transcendence of the current learning paradigm. As was done in Part 2 for CLCs, an Option Field is created, but the context is expanded to include a new learning system within which CLCs are grounded.

Chapter 10 is a statement of values and core ideas. It is written within the context of the knowledge base that was previously constructed and within the "option boundaries" that were chosen to design the future learning system.

Chapter 11 is the presentation of an image of a future learning system. It is restated and expanded upon in Chapter 12 as new knowledge, context, content, and methods for the future learning system. In Chapter 13, the image is evaluated by checking it against the design criteria.

Chapter 8: Initial Exploration

Vision of Society

Human evolution is moving at a faster pace than ever before. In *The Third Wave*, Alvin Toffler contends that human beings have experienced two kinds of historical waves—agricultural and industrial—and have now entered into a third wave that is often referred to as the information/knowledge age. It took humans fifty thousand years to advance through the hunting stage, ten thousand years to advance through the agricultural stage, five hundred years to advance through the industrial stage, and fifty years to advance through the post-industrial stage (Banathy 1996, 91). In earlier times it was not necessary for people to be competent in social systems design because of the long lag time between human evolutionary transitions. However, today the human race is advancing at a much faster rate than ever before, and with greater complexity, and it is necessary for citizens who are effected by these developments to participate in both individual and collective human development.

Because of the advent of technology, several societies are now experiencing an information explosion. Everyday new ideas and beliefs are being developed, disseminated, tested, evaluated, and revised by people from various locations around the globe using advanced technologies such as the Internet. This makes it necessary for individuals to participate in the design and redesign of their systems and properly guide humanity. If not, then a greater possibility exists for them to become victims of their own inability to change those systems in times when change is most necessary.

It is important for systems design to be part of educational programs. Before design can be thought of on a grand scale, a design culture needs to be created in which it can be learned as a subject and developed as a skill for citizenship. One way to create a design culture is through the use of "design incubators," which are referred to in this paper as *Inter-University Futures Collaboratives*. Within these Collaboratives students of design learn to create images of the future as well as test models of new systems that they create. The more images and models that are created, tested, and shared with those in the greater community, the more the global community will be prepared for uncertainties of the future.

But education in design or the creation of a new learning environment cannot be created without a vision of society and a vision of a future learning system. One vision of society could be…

A society in which every individual discovers his innate potential (true self) and lives a life that is commensurate with his self and others in order to, through participatory democratic actions, create a culture that develops and sustains the political, cultural, economic, and environmental spheres of society.

New Realities and Their Implications

In order to actualize a new vision of society, current realities and their implications need to be confronted. Though not a complete list, some realities include:

Cognitive and Human Growth Realities

- Fifty-percent of a child's neuron connections, or learning capacity, is developed by age five and an additional thirty-percent is developed by age eight.

- The more positive experiences a child has that are commensurate with his self, the more his brain's capacity will develop.

- A healthy diet is important for both brain growth and development.

- Each person's brain develops differently and at different rates.

- A learning slump occurs during the age of nine because of histological development activities, such as the differentiation of the two hemispheres of the brain.

Sociocultural Realities

- The environment is integral to the culture of a society; thus rising as the fourth sphere of societal affairs, the other three being political, cultural, and economic.

- It is now recognized that a society can function best when a harmonious and equitable relationship exists between the political, cultural, economic, and environmental spheres.

- A concept of democracy has re-arisen in the political sphere—participatory democracy. It empowers individuals to have a more active role in societal affairs.

- All spheres or sectors of society are now seen as educative and being directly tied to a community's learning environment.

Economic Realities

- Economies come to resemble more the ecology of organisms as they continue to exemplify the characteristics of interlinkage, coevolution, and constant flux.

- Information exchange in the economies is ubiquitous.

- Economies are moving from the production of material goods toward the creation of intellectual opportunities.

- Consumers have a greater stake in the production of the goods they consume and the services they receive—They are now "prosumers" (producer + consumer).

- Currency transactions are occurring electronically and ubiquitously.

- Digital markets are replacing physical markets.

- Wealth is created not in money but in opportunities—one new invention spawns several new inventions that generate a decentralized system of wealth.

Socio-technological Realities

- New technologies not only create complexity and chaos, but also are the tools for dealing with the complexity and chaos that they create.

- New technologies are breaking down all forms of barriers between people.

Technological Realities

- New technologies, such as "hydrogen fuel cells" or "plasma waste converters," are redefining energy needs.

- New technologies have allowed humanity to unlock the DNA code.

- New technologies have allowed humanity to better understand the universe.

- New technologies have the capacity to benefit humanity.

Scientific Realities

- Systems Thinking has replaced the Cartesian/Newtonian Paradigm.

- New insights into the universe support a more metaphysical viewpoint of human existence.

Organizational Realities

- New insights into systems thinking have given rise to new organizational concepts such as "transformational leadership," "learning organizations," and "capacities for transformation."

- The idea of "externalizing costs" onto society is giving way to new organizational concepts such as "ecological commerce," "natural capitalism," and "green manufacturing" in which costs are either internalized or designed out of the system of the organization.

Some Implications of the Realities

- A more learner-centered educational environment.

- Better diet for children and a change in the food supply.

- A transformation *in the relationship* between the four spheres of society in most, if not all, developed and developing nations.

- A transformation *within* each of the four spheres of society.

- A more citizen-centered political sphere.

- A more integrated cultural sphere.

- A more globally integrated economic sphere.

- A cleaner, more sustainable environment.

- A universal and digital monetary system.

- An increase in digital bartering.

- A recognition of universal human rights.

- A more decentralized energy system.

- The creation and empowerment of a "prosumer" class.

- The necessity of systemic design architecture for proper citizenship.

- Greater travel and cultural exchange between people.

- The resolution of many of humanity's biological and social ills.

Vision of a Future Learning System

These new realities and their implications allow a vision of a future learning system to be created. One vision of a future learning system could be…

An open and transformational learning environment that exists to

1) *Assist individuals with discovering and actualizing their innate potentials (true selves);*

2) *Transmit to individuals cultural roles;*

3) *Convey to individuals values of the culture;*

4) *Assist individuals in learning how to search for truth, beauty, and good, and to create value in the world;*

5) *Develop in individuals competency in the culture's notational systems;*

6) *Provide to individuals guidance, coaching, teaching, and training in the human domains of its society;*

7) *Nurture in individuals the capacity to continuously transform; and*

8) *Encourage experts in their respective fields to participate in the educational endeavor of the learning system.*

Chapter 9: Space 1: Transcending the Current Learning Paradigm

Creating an Option Field

Figure 1. Adaptation of Banathy's Option Field (1996, 63)

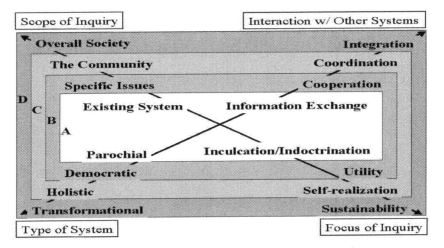

The visions and ideas that have been developed thus far give rise to the type of system that is to be employed. The choice is grounded in the values and core ideas that are articulated throughout the course of developing an option field, as shown in Figure 1. The options include Option A, Option B, Option C, and Option D. After a discussion of each option, the change dimensions are addressed in order to guide the choice. Finally, a choice is made and the reasons for the choice are articulated.

In addition, it should be noted that the discussion regarding the options are based upon the following assumptions:

● Learning across all educational systems is either grounded within the context of the learning/doing situation or decontextualized (or a mixture of the two).

● Learning across all educational systems has perennial purposes: "to transmit roles; to convey cultural values; to inculcate literacies; to communicate certain disciplinary content and ways of thinking...; [to] search within one's culture for what is true, what is beautiful, and what is good (Gardner 1999a, 35-36);" to create something of benefit for oneself and others (Bethel 1994); and to develop new capacities for an emerging society.

Option A: Exploration within the Existing System

Option A is exploration within the existing system, a parochial system. A parochial system is one in which principles, methods, and applications are strictly defined by the institution or the teachers (masters). The current public educational system in the U.S. is a parochial system. Another example includes religious schools where the pupil adheres to strict educational edicts for learning religious texts. The parochial system can also be found in the medieval apprenticeship where an apprentice enters into a formal relationship with a master. Another example of a parochial system is the modern centralized educational system where the State decides the educational principles and methods, and possibly the applications of instruction. Thus, the primary focus of a parochial system is the inculcation of values and beliefs and the indoctrination of a specific core of knowledge. Because of its narrow focus, the parochial system only interacts with other social systems through information exchange; there is no desire to develop special partnerships or relationships with systems that are far outside of its own realm.

Option B: Exploration of Specific Issues

Option B is the exploration of specific issues that affect the system. It is democratic because it calls for democratic participation by all of those members who are effected by the system's activities, such as teachers, parents, other organizations, and sometimes pupils. When specific issues need to be addressed, the system cooperates with other systems. Several private alternative schools, such as *New City School* in St. Louis, Missouri, have a democratic system of education. Another example is the New York City CUE CLC Program. As may be recalled, parents of the program empowered themselves to become more active in the affairs of the school. Some parents found themselves serving on a board of education, going to parent-teacher conferences, and taking a more active role in their children's learning.

Option C: Exploration Within the Community

Option C is the exploration and re-definition of community and is grounded in holistic educational principles (Flake 1993; Miller 1992):

- Education for human development
- Honoring students as individuals
- Learning through experience
- Emphasis on the wholeness of human experience
- Teacher as educator, coach, advisor, and friend
- Freedom of choice
- Education for participatory democracy
- Education for cultural diversity and global citizenship

- Education for earth literacy

- A spiritual worldview

In sum, Option C is the "self-realization" that should occur in education which educators such as John Dewey, Tsunesaburo Makiguchi, Henry Morris, and Frank Manley recognized and worked to achieve in their own educational experiments with schools in their communities.   In a holistic educational system the learner is the center of the universe and all learning principles, methods, and applications are in alignment with his cognitive abilities, learning needs, and learning desires.   Furthermore, other systems work in coordination with the holistic system.   For example, a school that is based upon the aforementioned holistic principles will coordinate its educational programs with organizations in the community, such as museums or botanical gardens.

Option D: Exploration Within the Overall Society

Option D is exploration within the overall society.   The educational system is transformational.   It recognizes the world realities and integrates itself into other systems so that it will be highly responsive to changes.   For example, instead of seeing the social issue of daycare as mutually exclusive from the educational issue of teacher training, the system of daycare is integrated into the system of teacher education.   The integration of these two systems allows them to act as a single system and view problem-situations systemically.

Change Dimensions

After constructing the Option Field, the next step is to create the Change Dimensions.   Figure 2 illustrates the change dimensions.

Figure 2. Bela Banathy's Change Dimensions (1996, 114)

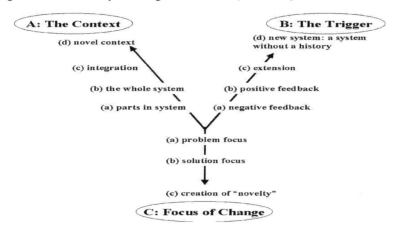

Table 1. Change Dimensions and Configurations (ibid., 115-117)

The Context Dimension	The Trigger Dimensions	Focus of Change
Model I Configuration: [A(a), B(a), C(a)]	Model V Configuration: [B(b), A(b), C(b)]	Model IX Configuration: [C(b), A(b)]
Model II Configuration: [A(b), B(b), C(b)]	Model VI Configuration: [B(c), A(b), C(c)]	Model X Configuration: [C(c), A(b)]
Model III Configuration: [A(c),B(c), C(c)]	Model VII Configuration: [B(a), A(a), C(a)]	
Model IV Configuration: [A(d), B(d), C(c)]	Model VIII Configuration: [C(a), B(a), C(a)]	

Configuration Models

Model I Configuration: This configuration views the context as a part of the system, just another cog in the greater machine. Change occurs when something goes wrong (negative feedback). If a cog breaks-down, then the purpose of change is to fix or replace it.

Model II Configuration: This configuration views the context as the whole system. If the environment changes (positive feedback), then the entire system must either be redesigned or replaced. For example, in office management, when e-mail and the Internet came into existence, traditional office management was altered. Instead of a worker being at his desk at 8:45 AM every morning, the system was redesigned in order to institute flex-time or on-line work so office efficiency would become better.

Model III Configuration: This configuration views the context of inquiry as extending into the greater environment. It calls for integrating the system with other systems, such as a school district integrating its elementary programs with museums, zoos, or local businesses.

Model IV Configuration: This configuration views the context as novelty, something that has no past.

Model V Configuration: This configuration views the trigger as positive feedback in which the whole system must be changed, similar to Model II Configuration.

Model VI Configuration: This configuration views the trigger as moving the boundaries of exploration beyond the system and integrating itself with other systems, similar to Model III Configuration.

Model VII Configuration: This configuration views the trigger as negative feedback, similar to Model I Configuration.   Again, something is wrong within the system and an attempt to change the broken cog is necessary.

Model VIII Configuration: This configuration is focused on the problem within the system, similar to Model I and VII Configurations.

Model IX Configuration: This configuration is focused on finding a solution to the design situation, the whole system is taken into account.   This is similar to Model II and V Configurations.

Model X Configuration: This configuration is focused on creating a new system without a history in a new environment.

Configuration Types

Type I Configuration: Type I consists of Models I, VII, and VIII and calls for change within the system, such as fixing the worn-out cogs of a machine.

Type II Configuration: Type II includes Models II, V, and IX and calls for the redesign of the whole system, such as replacing the horse-and-buggy with the automobile.

<u>Type III Configuration</u>: Type III consists of Models III and VI and calls for the integration of the system with other systems that are relevant to the activities of the system, such as integrating an elementary school program with museums, zoos, or local businesses.   This requires systems design.

<u>Type IV Configuration</u>: Type IV consists of Models VI and X and calls for the creation of a new system without a history that is to be designed within an entirely new environment.

Choosing an Option

For the purposes of this paper, Option D is chosen to be the most relevant option because of the desire to create a learning system that does not exist yet (Type IV Configuration), a transformational system. However, even though Option D has been selected, it does not exclude the dimensions of the other options. For instance, in Option C the holistic educational principles should also be found in Option D because these principles, as will be learned later, are compatible with a transformational system.

A transformational learning system is one that not only transforms the individual throughout each stage of his life, but also transforms the community as self-realizing individuals interact with one another. Furthermore, a transformational learning system works to maintain sustainability between the four spheres of society—political, cultural, economic, and environmental. Thus, learning happens within a holistic context[1], that is to say, learning occurs with the recognition of the complexity and interconnectedness of things and the significance of life in all its forms. The following statement of values and core ideas illustrates the philosophical foundations for the choice of Option D.

---

[1] For an example of transformational learning within a holistic context, see the University Corporation for Atmospheric Research (UCAR) website at http://www.windows.ucar.edu.

Chapter 10: Statement of Values and Core Ideas

The following principles and core ideas serve as the foundation for Option D.

Core Ideas for an Alternative Framework for CLCs in the 21st Century

1. Principles of Self-actualization

2. Principles of Brain-based Learning and Theory of Multiple Intelligences

3. Principles of Symbolic Interactionist Social Psychology

4. Principles of Self-Government

5. Principles of Learner-Centered, Learner-Directed Education

6. Principles of Systemic Design

Core Values for an Alternative Framework for CLCs in the 21st Century

The values that members of the learning system should believe in include:

1. Every individual is unique and should follow his "personal destiny."

2. Learning is a cognitive matter and best occurs when organized around the cognitive abilities of each individual in order to assist him with actualizing his inherent potential.

3. Learning is a personal and communal matter and best occurs when learners are encouraged to take control of their own learning and focus and reflect upon their own learning processes.

4. The world is a symbolic one and people continually *interact*—probe and test—with the environment within which they live in order to adjust harmoniously to its changes.

5. Social systems exist in order to guide a society's affairs.   Furthermore, all competent and able members of a community should share in the design of their social systems through participatory democratic measures.

6. The social systems that humans create are of a political, cultural, economic, and environmental nature and support the greater community when in harmony with one another.

Chapter 11: Image of a Future Learning System

Table 2 juxtaposes the image of a future learning system (transformational learning system) with the current public educational system in the United States (parochial educational system).

Table 2. Image of a Future Learning System

Image	Current System (Miller 1995)
Education should assist an individual with actualizing his potential.	Education serves the economic interests of the nation and employment needs of corporations.
Education should be organized around the cognitive abilities of each individual.	Education is organized around empirical, analytical, intellectual, and utilitarian knowledge.
Education should encourage learners to take control of their own learning and focus and reflect upon their own learning processes.	Teachers are professionals and students are their clients, and teachers should control the students' learning.
Education should assist individuals with interacting with the environment within which they live so they can adjust harmoniously to its changes.	The school building is the best location for learning and adequately prepares students for today's needs.
Education should assist learners with becoming competent and able community members who, through participatory democratic measures, systemically design their own social systems.	School administrators, elected officials, and bureaucrats know best what teachers, children, and the community need in terms of an education.
Education should strive to maintain the sustainable relationship between the political, cultural, economic, and environmental sectors of society.	Education is primarily a political matter.
Education should strive to promote democratic values via participatory democracy and free market mechanisms.	Democratic values are best promoted by the majority control of state schooling and its revenues.

Chapter 12: Space 2: New Knowledge, Context, Content, and Methods

In creating the image of a future learning system, it is pertinent to include new knowledge, context, content, and methods. Those basic principles that have been included as the core ideas are more explicitly identified in this chapter.

Principles of Self-Actualization

Self-actualization/self-realization has been employed in this paper without much elaboration on its meaning. In this section some of the fundamental principles of self-actualization that have been developed over the centuries by scholars in fields such as philosophy, psychology, and education are identified. To follow is an abbreviated list of principles of self-actualization.

First Principle: *Self-actualization only occurs if basic needs and preconditions have been met first.* Psychologists acknowledge that self-actualization is the peak of human experiences and for it to occur, certain basic needs are required. Abraham Maslow in *Motivation and Personality*, has created a "Hierarchy of Needs" that lists the preconditions in the following order: freedom, physiological needs, safety needs, belongingness and love needs, esteem needs, and then self-actualization (1987, 22).

Second Principle: *Self-actualization occurs not in socio-psychological isolation but within the contexts of "antecedent sociality" and "consequent sociality."* David Norton, a leading figure in normative individualism, recognizes that all individuals when born into society receive some form of enculturation and cannot actualize their potentials without a "moral starting point." He refers to this as *antecedent sociality—*

"a received sociality to which the person (as child and adolescent) is responsible" (1976, 253). The other kind of sociality, *consequent sociality*, is "a constituted sociality for which he [the individual] shares responsibility" (ibid.). Therefore, it is through the process of becoming what one is potentially that the individual contributes to the actualization of other individuals and vice-versa.

Third Principle: *Self-actualization is guided by a set of virtues in human cultures.* Scholars in several disciplines, such as philosophers David Norton (1976), Alasdair MacIntyre (1984), and Charles Taylor (1989, 1991) and educational scholars such as John Dewey (1908, 1972), Tsunesaburo Makiguchi (in Bethel 1989), Ernest L. Boyer (1995), and Howard Gardner (1999a) recognize the importance that a set of virtues plays in society. A virtue is *a distinctive disposition of character that serves as utility for one's self-actualization; defines and sustains the intrinsic goods of one's profession which in effect helps to further the actualization of the self; and sustains the traditions that provide the context for both individual lives and professions to develop.*

Fourth Principle: *Self-actualization occurs only in mature people.* Both Maslow and Norton argue that self-actualization occurs only in mature people. They make a distinction between self-actualization and growth toward it. Maslow in a study of three thousand college students on self-actualization concluded that self-actualization does not occur in young people or in children. They "have not yet achieved identity, or autonomy, nor have they had time enough to experience an enduring, loyal, post-romantic love relationship, nor have they generally found their calling, the altar upon which to offer themselves" (1987, 126). Similarly, Norton from a philosophical perspective asserts that each life has four stages: childhood, adolescence, maturity, and old age, and that every life proceeds through each incommensurable stage (1976). Childhood and adolescence are stages that have not yet actualized the inner potential of the individual. Childhood is a "nature subsisting for the most part in the mode of a potentiality whose time for actualization is not yet" (ibid., 172); and adolescence is self-discovery—"I am an authentic living being, not a derivation. From this moment forward it is I myself who must do my living" (ibid., 179). In addition to childhood and adolescence, old age is not a stage of self-actualization since it is "pure deterioration, thereby contradicting the basic self-actualization thesis" (ibid., 159).

Fifth Principle: *Children and youth can only achieve self-actualization through "good-growth-toward-self-actualization."* In order for people to become mature, self-actualizing individuals, society must develop its cultural institutions around people (Dewey 1990, 1997a; Norton 1976; Gardner 1993a, 1993b, 1999a, 1999b). This calls for a new concept of learning as David Clark (1996), John Dewey (1997a, 1997b), Abraham Maslow (1989, xiv), and David Norton (1976, 349) champion. Society should assist children with their growth toward self-actualization by providing them equal access to resources that are commensurate with their growth (Maslow 1987, xiv; Taylor 1991, 50; Norton 1976, 324; Gates 2001; Jefferson 1999, III.16: 185-191). Furthermore, parents and adults cannot have any preconceptions about what a person should be or should become. This is what Norton refers to as a fallacy of anachronism—"the imposition of a set of principles, truths, and/or moral terms of one stage upon another incommensurable stage (1976, 161).

Sixth Principle: *"Good-growth-toward-self-actualization" is a process that is based upon an ideal of "desert," that is, one receiving what is due to him and doing what is his to do.* This principle addresses the issue of justice that Western philosophers, such as Aristotle in *Nicomachean Ethics*, have addressed for centuries. Charles Taylor explains the principle as that of "fairness, which demands equal chances for everyone to develop their own identity, which include—as we can now understand more clearly—the universal recognition of difference, in whatever modes this is relevant to identity" (1989, 59). Thomas Jefferson in a letter to John Adams dated October 28, 1813 resonates with this ideal and notes that a law in the Virginia State Legislature was passed in order to abolish "the privilege of primogeniture" and divide "the lands of intestates equally among all their children, or other representatives." William H. Gates, Sr. in his speech to the National Press Club on the topic of the Estate Tax echoes Jefferson's sentiments and places the ideal in terms of self-realization—"A good life should be something that is achieved, it should not be delivered as a result of the womb that you start out in."

Principles of Brain-Compatible Learning and Theory of Multiple Intelligences

In the educational community today, brain-compatible learning is becoming the science upon which understandings of learning and human growth are founded. Brain-compatible learning finds its roots in neuroscience which is itself a synergy of disciplines: chemistry, immunology, biology, pharmacology, computational sciences, medicine, systems thinking, and artificial intelligence modeling (Jensen 1998a, 2). The learning theories, methods, and applications that are developed for brain-compatible learning are developed out of the knowledge that comes from Functional Magnetic Resonance Imaging, lab experiments with animals, Computerized Electrodes (EEG and MEG), clinical studies, Positron Emission Tomography, autopsies, and spectrometers (ibid., 7-8). Furthermore, in discussing brain-compatible learning, Howard Gardner's Theory of Multiple Intelligences should also be acknowledged. He defines an intelligence as, "a biopsychological potential to process information that can be activated in a cultural setting to solve problems or create products that are of value in a culture" (1999b, 34). Based upon these findings, the following fundamental principles of brain-compatible learning have been ascertained (Blythe 1998; Caine and Caine 1994; Dryden 1995; Dryden and Rose 1995; Gardner 1993, 1999b; Jensen 1998a, 1998b, 2000; Maier 1969; Maslow 1989; Tishman, Perkins, and Jay 1995; Werner 1948).

- *The brain processes information in a parallel fashion.*
- *When people learn the entire physiology is engaged.*
- *The search for meaning and understanding is an innate ability.*

- *Emotions are critical to learning in that they drive attention, health, meaning, memory, and survival.*

- *Genes, nutrition, peers, brain dysfunction, prior learning, experience, and temperament and character all influence learning.*

- *Parts and wholes can be processed simultaneously by the brain.*

- *Focused attention and peripheral perception are both aspects of learning.*

- *Conscious and unconscious processes are both aspects of learning.*

- *Spatial memory and rote learning memory are two kinds of systems used by the brain.*

- *Embedded facts and experiences in natural spatial memory help people remember better.*

- *Stressful situations cause the brain to act in survival mode at the expense of higher order learning.*

- *Each brain is unique and developmental stages vary between children.*

- *The brain has the capacity to grow new neural connections at any age.*

- *A variety of pathways are available in the brain for the storage of information and experiences.*

- *Movement, foods, attention cycles, and drugs and chemicals affect learning.*

- *Intelligence is valued within the context of society.*

- *Experience causes the brain to adapt to various situations.*

Principles of Symbolic Interactionist Social Psychology

In alignment with the principles of self-actualization and the principles of brain-compatible learning are the principles of symbolic interactionism. Like the eudaimonistic thinkers and brain-compatible scientists and practitioners, symbolic interactionists recognize the significance of *meaning*. When an individual goes about self-actualization, he defines the *meaning* of his existence and works toward the actualization of that existence. When the brain processes information, the information can only become long-term memory when it is learned within a *meaningful* context. When people do things, according to symbolic interactionist social psychology, they do them according to meaning, and meaning "is derived from, or arises out of, the social interaction that one has with one's fellows" (Blumer 1969, 2). Based upon a survey of some of the leading figures in symbolic interactionist social psychology—Howard S. Becker and Michael M. McCall (1990), Herbert Blumer (1969), Joel M. Charon (1998), John P. Hewitt (1997), and George Herbert Mead (1967, 1972)—the principles of symbolic interactionism are restated in the following manner.

- *The central task of symbolic interactionist social psychology is not to focus on the individual and his idiosyncrasies but to focus on how individuals interact socially and how those social interactions are formed.*

- *Human actions occur as a result of the way people create and maintain meaning and how they define situations. Thus people act with plans and purposes whether they are covert or overt.*

- *Meaning can be transformed.*

144

- *The individual can solely recognize meaning or it can be shared.*

- *Human action is self-referential and is caused not only by interaction with others but interaction with the self.*

- *Human conduct and unexpected human events are not the result of "an invisible hand," but occur as people interact with one another.*

- *Society and culture shape human conduct but society and culture are also the products of human conduct.*

Principles of Self-Government

In order to create an alternative framework for community learning centers, the political sphere should also be explored. The type of government that is advocated in this treatise is democratic "self-government." The principles of self-actualization, principles of brain-compatible learning and theory of multiple intelligences, and principles of symbolic interactionist social psychology are antecedent to the principles of democratic self-government because they provide the foundation from which good democratic self-government rises and the framework within which it operates. For brevity purposes, the perennial thought on self-government as developed by key thinkers such as Socrates, Plato, Aristotle, Thomas Hobbes, John Locke, Thomas Jefferson, Alexis de Tocqueville, and John Dewey is distilled into the following list of principles and conditions.

PRINCIPLES

First Principle: *Government closest to the people is government best for the people!* Thomas Jefferson writes in a letter to William Charles Jarvis, "I know no safe depository of the ultimate powers but the people themselves" (1999, VI.13: 381-382). In alignment with this thinking, it is reasserted that the people are the best source for governing themselves. A direct, participatory, and when needed, representative form of government should be established; and within the cultural sphere the people should govern themselves through their own private and civil associations.

Second Principle: *An enlightened electorate enlightens!* Also in his letter to William Charles Jarvis, Jefferson writes, "If we think them [the people] not enlightened enough to exercise their control with wholesome discretion, the remedy is not to take it from them, but to inform their discretion by education" (ibid.).   This goes to the heart of a transformational learning system.   It is a person's right and obligation to control one's own mind.   As a right, government must first and foremost protect it in order for society itself to be free and to enlighten.   Locke emphasizes this argument in, *Two Treatises of Government*, when he discusses Man's state as that of a "State of perfect Freedom" (Chapter II, Section 4, 1988, 269).   As an obligation, he must do his utmost for himself and his fellows to govern his own affairs and not have the State do it for him. He should become a productive member of society and participate in its progress.   As Tocqueville contends, only a tyrannical form of government likes for its "citizens to enjoy themselves provided that they think only of enjoying themselves" and to think of nothing else (2000, 663).

Third Principle: *Equity is most equitable when it's horizontal!*   Services that are funded by the public require two layers of horizontal equity.   The first layer is horizontal equity between taxpayers and the second layer is horizontal equity between users of public services.   Vermont at the beginning of its statehood recognized these two layers of horizontal equity as well as their relationship to, what Vermont identifies as its most important public service, education.   In 1777 the Vermont constitutional architects ratified Chapter II, Section 40, which in today's Vermont Constitution is Chapter II, Section 68.   It establishes that "Laws for the encouragement of virtue and prevention of vice and immorality ought to be constantly kept in force, and duly executed; and a competent number of schools ought to be maintained in each town." Furthermore, it establishes in Chapter I, Article 7, a common benefits clause so that all individuals have equal access and opportunities to public services. The clause states, "That government is, or ought to be, instituted for the common benefit…of the people, nation, or community, and not for the particular emolument or advantage of any single person, family, or set of persons." The common benefits and education clauses are necessary in any transformational learning community so that horizontal equity exists between taxpayers for and users of publicly funded services.

Fourth Principle: *Sustain not what is might, but what is right!* When considering the idea of sustainability in this paper, society should be thought of in terms of four spheres—political, cultural, economic, and environmental—that interact synergistically with one another. *Social Sustainability* is the condition by which society maintains the complementarity and congeniality of personal excellences between its members that in turn transforms the society from one generation to the next. The political sphere is government. In order to have a sustainable political system, government should do those things that private and civil associations are unable to do, such as levy taxes and protect civil liberties and private property. The cultural sphere consists of private and civil associations as well as those public institutions that the political body has created to support the cultural sphere. It has an obligation to perform the communal tasks necessary for sustaining the whole society. The economic sphere consists of the "market." Principles of self-actualization and the antecedent principles of self-government guide the market's members. The environment includes the natural environs. Humanity has the capacity to live in a world without violence to itself and the planet. Therefore, society as a whole should explore ways in creating sustainable functions and components that operate synergistically with the environment.

CONDITIONS

<u>First Condition</u>: *Only self-actualizing individuals can be entrusted to govern the affairs of others.*   One problem that modern self-government encounters is the dilemma of moral minimalism—Anyone who is a citizen has a right to govern and laws are established to protect people from harming one another (Norton 1991, 21).   However, in a self-actualizing society, self-government incorporates a standard for governance. David Norton refers to this standard as *noblesse oblige*—"Greater moral responsibility attends greater moral development" (ibid., 150).   *Noblesse Oblige* also implies that those individuals who are capable of governing their own affairs should be entrusted to govern the affairs of the community.   This does not mean creating an elite class living separately from others in the community or employing a litmus test for those who wish to serve.   In a society of self-actualizing individuals, all mature members are sufficiently well qualified to govern the affairs of those who are not governing since each member is equal in loving the common good.

<u>Second Condition</u>: *Governance operates in accordance with The Principle of Equal Consideration and The Principle of Equality.*   Ian Morris in, "The Strong Principle of Equality and the Archaic Origins of Greek Democracy," refers to Robert Dahl's definition of Athenian self-government in understanding these two principles (1996, 20). Freedom does not spring from equality.   People are not first equal and then free, but are free and equal.   Freedom entitles people to develop into self-actualizing individuals. Equality entitles them to those goods that assist in achieving their self-actualization. Furthermore, in achieving a state of self-actualization, people are also equal in their ability to participate in the affairs of state and to make collective decisions.   This is

what is meant by the Principle of Equal Consideration.   The Principle of Equality makes it explicit that since each mature person is equal in his ability to participate in governance, then some persons are able to make some decisions for the whole community.

Third Condition: *Governance is an Obligation; it is neither a Right nor a Compact.* Unlike Hobbes and Locke who contend that governance is a compact entered upon in agreement or a right guaranteed to all men, under the principles of self-actualization it is an obligation (Jefferson 1999, IV.19: 286-287; Norton 1991, 99-100, 150; Yarbrough 1998, 20-26).   As a right, people can choose not to exercise the right of participation in governance.   A right asks very little of individuals in the way of participating as full members of society.   However, within the realm of *noblesse oblige*, an obligation asks the very best of all individuals.   This implies that all members have an obligation to themselves and to others to participate in the governance of the affairs of community as they are proceeding through their own self-actualization.   Governance cannot be left to those who do not yet exhibit the noble qualities of one's community.

Fourth Condition: *Self-Government lives in the light of the virtues.*   People are alike in achieving the virtues of their community, but qualitatively different in the way each does so (Aristotle, Politics, Book II, Section 2; Hansen 1996, 91-94; Morris 1996, 21-22; Wallach 1996, 331-332).   In governing the affairs of community, people should perform those duties that they are best qualified to perform.   Within this framework, citizenship is membership in governance as well as service.   For the betterment of the individual and his community, equality within the *polis* should be distributed in accordance with one's nature and abilities so he is able to govern himself and others best.

Fifth Condition: *Government should be thought of as a modern "metrioi."*   A *metrioi* is a community of "middling people" who think of themselves as part of a community of restrained, sensible individuals who are all of the same mind, *homonia*, and whose bonds are kept together through brotherly love, *philia* (Morris 1996, 21-22; Wallach 1996, 331-332).   All are alike in loving the greater good of the community but are qualitatively different in achieving it.   In a society of *metrioi* each person spurs on the self-realization of others by doing the work that is his to do in the *polis*.   He wishes for the best in all individuals so he too can achieve his best (Aristotle, Politics, Book II, Section 2; Hansen 1996, 91-94; Morris 1996, 21-22; Wallach 1996, 331-332).   Within the *metrioi* no separation of class exists because of profession, family, or caste.

Principles of Learner-Centered, Learner-Directed Education

It has been established in this paper that education should be learner-centered as well as learner-directed. This hypothesis is reformulated as an outline of fundamental principles for learning.

LEARNER-CENTERED EDUCATION

<u>First Principle</u>: *Learning starts with where the learner is cognitively.* Every learner is born with different capacities for learning. In addition, the environment within which the learner is raised influences his capacity to learn. Recognizing these two truths, learning must begin at the point of the learner's position in the world.

<u>Second Principle</u>: *Learning starts with the learner's interests.* Each learner has his own interests toward learning. These interests should be acted upon and guided by parents, teachers, mentors, and/or peers. Each act is considered learning within the realm of education since each act builds upon future commensurable acts that are governed by the Principle of Continuity, to which Dewey refers in, *Experience and Education*.

<u>Third Principle</u>: *Learning starts with connecting the learner to community.* A dichotomy between formal and informal learning does not exist. Activities *in* community are just as equal in importance as activities in formal learning environments since all acts are considered acts of learning. Furthermore, learners strive to understand what is true, beautiful, and good within their community.

Fourth Principle: *Learning starts with forming thinking dispositions.* In order to become self-directed learners and active participants in a democratic society, learners should develop dispositions toward thinking. Thinking dispositions are those "inclinations and habits of mind that benefit productive thinking…ongoing, abiding tendencies in thinking behavior exhibited over time across diverse thinking situations" (Tishman et al. 1995, 37). These dispositions consist of being curious and questioning, thinking broadly and adventurously, reasoning clearly and carefully, organizing one's thinking, and giving thinking time (ibid., 41-42).

LEARNER-DIRECTED EDUCATION

First Principle: *Learning starts with developing learning skills in the learner.* Learner-directed education is fostered within the individual over the course of time. In order to develop such skills, the learner should be provided with a learning environment that is democratic and free, where there is horizontal equity and access to those resources that support one's self-realization. Over the course of time and via the interactions with peers and mentors, he develops the necessary skills to be an informed and self-directed learner and a participant in the democratic experiment.

Second Principle: *Learning starts with directing one's learning in interaction with other learners.* Self-direction occurs in interaction with other individuals. The learner can direct his learning when it is in accordance with the Principles of Congeniality and Complementarity of Excellences. Norton defines the Principle of Congeniality as a condition of friendship that "is neither pure resemblance nor pure difference, but is instead the 'congeniality' that obtains between persons who are alike in loving the good, but different in respect to the particular good each loves" (1976, 306-307). Complementarity of Excellences is when the individual uses his identity to complement the actualization of other individuals and to foster community, contribute to it, make it greater than it currently is for the common good of all (ibid., 10-13). Throughout the learning process the learner receives feedback on his learning from teachers, parents, and fellow learners. This feedback helps him assess his self-directed learning efforts. It signals to him if he is learning what he should be learning, if he understands what he is learning, and if he is learning it in a way that builds upon his future acts. This vital synergism between learner, peers, teachers, and parents is an important aspect of learner-directed education and the formation of self-actualizing individuals.

Principles of Systemic Design

In Part 2 the method of systems design architecture was addressed. Systems design was defined as "*A community of self-actualizing individuals, that is, a group of people who mutually share common values, interests, ideals, and knowledge that is germane to the system to be created, and who, through participatory democratic actions, creatively design meaningful systems that are shared with the greater community toward the guidance of human evolutionary development and the direction of positive social development.*" Furthermore, it was concluded that the purposes of systems design are to have the ability to 1) deal with complexity and chaos and 2) understand and participate in the design of social systems. It was also established that design should be done when the realities, beliefs, and values of the community are no longer commensurate with the social system that is serving them. Thus, models of a future desired system are created, chosen, and tested in order to decipher which should serve as the most ideal model for the future system. The design of the new system is done by a *community of self-actualizing individuals*—individuals who embody the attributes of confidence and courage, situational sensitivity, flexibility, tolerance, interactive movement, and management. The principles of systemic design that are adhered to in the design of an alternative framework for community learning centers include the following.

First Principle: *Design is a community of self-actualizing individuals who, through participatory democratic actions, creatively design meaningful systems that are shared with the greater community toward the guidance of human evolutionary development and the direction of positive social development.*

155

Second Principle: *Design is pursued so communities can better address complexity and chaos and understand and participate in the design of their social systems.*

Third Principle: *Design is pursued when the realities, beliefs, and values of the community are no longer commensurate with the social system that is serving them.*

Fourth Principle: *The product of design should be a model of the desired future social system.*

Fifth Principle: *The participants of design should be individuals who embody the attributes of confidence and courage, situational sensitivity, flexibility, tolerance, interactive movement, and management.*

Chapter 13: Space 4: Evaluation of Image

The task of creating new knowledge, context, content, and methods is now complete. It has been determined that the image is the correct one since it is commensurate with the below criteria.

Criteria

√ Vision of Society

√ Vision of Future Learning System

√ Core Values

√ Fundamental Principles

      Self-Actualization

      Brain-Compatible Learning and Theory of Multiple Intelligences

      Symbolic Interactionist Social Psychology

      Self-Government

      Learner-Centered, Learner-Directed Education

      Systemic Design

It is concluded that the image is in alignment with the criteria that have been established. The first part of the image addresses the issue of self-actualization: Every person is unique and has something to contribute to society.

The second part of the image recognizes fundamental truths of cognitive development and human growth. Even though each person is fundamentally comprised of the same organic tissue, each is qualitatively different in that all grow and learn at different rates and in different ways.

The third part of the image embraces the idea of self-directed learning and thinking. No individual can become a self-actualizing person if he is unable to direct his own learning. Furthermore, this self-direction does not occur in isolation and requires people to complement one another's learning in a congenial manner.

The fourth part of the image contends that learning occurs within the context of learning-in-community. Each activity in life is a learning activity and those activities that happen outside of formalized learning and those that are part of formalized learning should not be discriminated. Furthermore, learning activities should be organized in a manner of continuity that is commensurate with one's learning abilities, styles, as well as subject content and context.

By becoming self-directed learners, members of the learning community also become potential social systems designers. Self-directed learning is a voluntary participatory experience that embraces the ideals of self-government and self-renewal. Only self-directed learners can become competent members of the actively participatory democratic process of social systems design.

The sixth part of the image accepts the notion that education is paramount in creating a sustainable society. The task of education in community sustainability is the development and maintenance of a democratic community led by individuals of *noblesse oblige*. A democratic community is one that has a synergistic relationship between government and the private and civil associations of the community. Self-actualizing individuals lead this sustainability effort since they are the only true individuals who can be entrusted by the community with the noble task of government and leading and/or facilitating the effort to maintain the synergy between the political, cultural, economic, and environmental spheres of society

Finally, education strives to promote the democratic values of participatory democracy and free market mechanisms. Democracy should be practiced by individuals of all ages within all facets of society. When democracy and education are spoken of, *democracy-in-education* is what is meant. Democracy is learned via the social interactions between people. Furthermore, education promotes free market mechanisms. One way this can occur is through a decentralized system in which learners use vouchers or passes for teachers and learning centers that foster personal growth and development. If a learner does not like his learning situation, he should be able to opt out of it for a better one in the free market of learning resources. The State cannot be entrusted to monopolize and allot educational services and resources because it is not responsible for moral and personal development. In a democratic society such as our own, people are entrusted to govern their own lives and live out their lives as they wish in relationship with their community and the common good. In terms of learning, the State's role is to be a conducive power for self-realization, and one way to do so is to ensure the proper and equitable use of free market mechanisms such as learning vouchers or passes.

Part 4

A New Design Solution for CLCs

Creating an Alternative Framework for the 21ˢᵗ Century

Introduction

Part 3 was the creation of a new knowledge base that included alternative values, core ideas, and an image of a future learning system.   Part 4, therefore, is the creation of an alternative learning framework.   Designing community learning centers without a framework is similar to designing a living room without a house.   It is within this new framework that community learning centers become more effective in helping to create sustainable communities for life in the twenty-first century.

To assist in creating an alternative learning framework, Banathy's Core Definition Spiral is used.   As illustrated in Figure 1, there are in the model four spirals: Core Definition Spiral, Specifications Spiral, Functions Model Spiral, and the Model of Enabling Systems Spiral.

Figure 1.   Adaptation of Banathy's Core Definition Spiral (1991, 178)

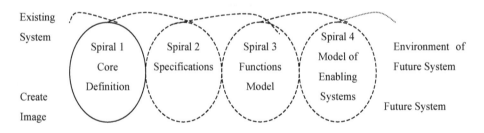

In Chapter 14 a core definition of the new learning system is developed. This core definition is comprised of the mission and purposes. Four different definitions of learning systems are provided and the one that most appropriately reflects the image of the future learning system is chosen. Furthermore, the core definition for community learning centers is re-evaluated in order to determine if it is in alignment with the core definition for the new learning system.

After choosing a core definition, the specifications for the learning system are developed in Chapter 15. Specifically addressed are users, services and their characteristics, ownership, responsibilities of a learning network, and the learning system's relationship with government, community, and individuals. The specifications are then evaluated in order to determine if they adequately reflect the core definition of the new learning system. In other words, does the system have the parts necessary to do what it is designed to do?

Chapter 16 addresses the functions of a learning network. Banathy argues that in designing functions the following questions should be addressed (1996, 76):

- What are the key functions that have to be carried out that enable the system to attain its mission and meet its specifications?

- How do these functions interact to constitute a system of functions?

- What are the subfunctions and how do they integrate into subsystems of key functions?

- What are the component functions of subfunctions?

- How can we organize the subfunctions in subsystems of functions?

161

In Chapter 17 the enabling systems are designed. These consist of the management system, organization system, and the systemic environment (For clarity purposes, I refer to systemic environment as "implementation.") (ibid.). The management system ensures that the implementation of the system's functions will operate as they are designed to operate in the functions model (ibid., 140). The organizational system determines how organizational and staff capacity will be created in order to carry out the tasks as described in the functions model (ibid.). The systemic environment embeds the learning system that is designed (ibid., 141).

Finally, the new learning system is presented in Chapter 18 as a model of three relationships: systems-environment model, functions/structure model, and process/behavioral model. The systems-environment model is a bird's-eye view of the model in that it observes the relational arrangements and dynamics between the different systems and the environment (ibid., 79). The functions/structure model is a snapshot view. It observes the system at a given moment in time in order to see what the system is and what it does (ibid., 80). The process/behavioral model is a motion picture view since it observes the behavior of the system throughout time (ibid.).

Chapter 14: Spiral 1: Core Definition of a Future Learning System

The purpose of the first spiral is to develop a core definition that adequately reflects the image of the future learning system so that it can serve as a framework for community learning centers. In developing a core definition, the mission and purposes of the system are identified. Four kinds of definitions based upon four possible kinds of learning systems have been developed: Parochial System, Democratic System, Holistic System, and Transformational System. Table 1 depicts the four definitions as they relate to each system.

Table 1. Mission Statements for Four Possible Kinds of Learning Systems

Elements of System	**Option 1** Parochial System (Modern State)	**Option 2** Democratic System	**Option 3** Holistic System	**Option 4** Transformational System
Learners and Community	Operate as separate entities. Community is "something out there" and learning is "something in the school" and occurs in large classes with school-sanctioned textbooks and materials. Learners have little or no say in choosing course of study.	Operate on the basis of democratic participation and call for all of those members who are affected by the school's activities to participate in its decision-making processes. The community works as a partner with the school only at the level of issue resolution. Learners are empowered to take a more active role in learning and civic duty.	Operate on the basis of holistic educational principles within the context of the school. Learning is focused on the learner and the community works as a partner with the school in helping learners to achieve individual learning goals.	Operate within the framework of a community learning network so that learners of all ages have access to learning resources and arrangements throughout the entire community and that they may be assisted in actualizing their true potentials.
Environment	Closed	Design, develop, and offer programs and arrangements that create an enlightened electorate so all can contribute to the greater democratic community.	Design, develop, and offer programs and arrangements that integrate the environment into the learning experience so "good-growth-toward-self-	Encourage the creation of a true learning society in which all individuals contribute to the learning of others in their community despite

			actualization" can occur.	geographical differences.
Other Systems	Closed	Work with government agencies in achieving federal, state or district educational goals.	Work with other systems in achieving the learning goals of the learner.	Integrate functions and components of various social systems in order to achieve the learning goals of individual learners.
Its Members	Develop a learning community that focuses on achieving the "basics" of education. Hires teachers as servants of the State who report directly to a Principal and School Board.	Develop a learning community that encourages learners to become more active participants in their own learning as well as their civic duties.	Develop a learning community in which learners, parents, teachers, and administrators are working in concert for the greater good of the school.	Develop a learning community in which all members participate and contribute to the greater good of learning and becoming human.
Itself	Become a system that works cooperatively with teachers and others within the school.	Become a system that works cooperatively with learners and other social agencies in achieving educational goals.	Become a system that works cooperatively with parents, teachers, and administrators in order to meet learners' educational goals.	Become a transformational system in which individuals transform themselves daily, from the mental to the spiritual.

Table 1 provides a comparison between the different kinds of learning systems and their mission statements.   The kind of learning system within which CLCs shall operate is a transformational system.   A key difference between the holistic system and the transformational system is the relationships between the components.   In a holistic system learning is still considered to occur within a school climate.   Though learning is focused on the learner and his self-actualization, the arrangements among the school, the community, and environment are *partnership arrangements* not ***network relationships***, and this limits the possibilities of "good-growth-toward-self-actualization."   Within a partnership both organizations are separate and distinct entities that work together in achieving their own goals at well-defined levels of partnership involvement.   However, a network operates according to those rules that Kevin Kelly discusses in *New Rules for the New Economy: Radical Strategies for a Connected World*.   He purports that within a network organizations work to "feed the web first" so that they may maximize the value of the entire network (1998, 65-82). Thus, within a community learning network or a transformational learning system organizations and agencies integrate themselves into one another's system in order to provide the maximum benefit for all members of the network.   Furthermore, individuals have a greater possibility of actualizing their true selves within a community learning network than in a holistic system because of the law of plentitude: "In a network, the more opportunities that are taken, the faster new opportunities arise" (ibid., 45).   In other words, the more opportunities exist for individuals to complement their excellences within a culture of congeniality, then the greater the chances of those individuals to actualize their potential excellences.

In sum, the mission of the future learning system can be restated as follows:

- Become a community learning network that is able to maximize the greatest benefits for individuals in their development toward self-actualization.
- Provide for learners of all ages an array of learning arrangements, relationships, and resources so they can actualize their fullest human potentials.
- Encourage the creation of a true learning society in which all individuals are able to contribute to the learning of others in their community despite geographical differences.

- Integrate functions and components of various social systems in order to achieve the learning goals of individual learners.

- Develop a learning community in which all members are able to participate and contribute to the greater good of learning and becoming human.

- Become a transformational learning system in which individuals are transforming themselves daily, from the mental to the spiritual.

In addition to the mission statement, it is necessary to provide a statement regarding the arrangements and relationships within the community learning network. This statement is the Purposes and is provided as follows:

- Create a society in which all spheres of society—political, cultural, economic, and environmental—are arranged and integrated to assist individuals with actualizing their true potentials.

- Organize learning principles, methods, applications, and strategies around the cognitive abilities, interests, and inclinations of each learner.

- Encourage learners to take an active role in their own learning by providing them guidance and support in self-directed learning and self-assessment.

- Provide learners opportunities to interact with their environment and society so they can understand it better and become more apt at adjusting to its changes.

- Provide learners a wide range of experiences in self-government so they share in the design of their social systems through participatory democratic measures.

- Strive to maintain the sustainable relationship between the political, cultural, economic, and environmental spheres.

- Promote democratic values via democratic self-rule and free market mechanisms within the learning system.

In addition to the mission and purposes, the core definition of a community learning center should be re-evaluated in order to determine if it is in alignment with the system. In designing a CLC or "node" of a learning system, it is important that it and the framework are compatible with one another and be based upon common principles so that they operate synergistically. The mission for a community learning center has been adjusted and is re-stated as follows:

- Become a "node" in the network that helps to facilitate learning and network relationships in order to maximize the total benefits of the learning network.
- Provide for learners of all ages learning resources and arrangements that assist them in actualizing their true potentials.
- Encourage the creation of a true learning society in which all individuals are able to contribute to one another's learning despite geographical differences.
- Integrate functions with other learning organizations or human services, such as museums.
- Develop a learning community in which all are able to participate and contribute to the greater good of learning and becoming human.
- Become a transformational system in which individuals are transforming themselves daily, from the mental to the spiritual.

Space 4: Evaluation of Core Definition

In conclusion, the alternative learning framework is in alignment with the image since it is a restatement of that image in mission form. Furthermore, the mission of the CLC is in alignment with the mission of the alternative learning system after adding to the CLC Mission, "Become a 'node' in the network that helps to facilitate learning and network relationships in order to maximize the total benefits of the learning network." Network relationships are different from partnership arrangements and the nature of the CLC should be clarified within the framework of the learning network.

Space 2: Core Definition as New Knowledge

The core definition of the future learning system as expressed in the mission statement and purposes is now new knowledge. Referring to Banathy's Design Architecture on page 108, it was created as a result of the interaction between exploration (Space 1) and design (Space 3) and a comparison between the parochial, democratic, holistic, and transformational mission statements. Having decided upon the mission statement, the purposes of the system were defined. The mission statement was then compared (Space 4) with the mission statement of the CLC. As a result of this comparison, *partnership arrangements* and *network relationships* could be distinguished better. This gave way to an adjustment in the CLC mission statement (Space 3). The phrase, "Become a 'node' in the network that helps to facilitate learning and network relationships in order to maximize the total benefits of the learning network" was added since the CLC should exhibit the nature of a "node."

As for purposes of a CLC, this question cannot be answered here because it solely depends upon the exact nature of the CLC. In *The Whitepaper* of the International CLC Network, the group identified several patterns of CLCs: the community garden, the community kitchen, the community media & technology center, the community network center, the community arts center, the community science center, a center for bioregional awareness, and agricultural entrepreneurship and telecenters. Each of these centers has the mission as noted above, but their purposes are different. It becomes the task of each community to determine which kinds of CLCs are best for its community and design those centers so their functions or services may be integrated.

Chapter 15: Spiral 2: Specifications of a Future Learning Network

In this chapter a statement of specifications is formulated. This statement and the core definition are the primary components for the system's requirements that are used in designing the learning network. The statement of specifications addresses the following questions:

- Who are the users? What are their responsibilities?

- Who owns the Network and to whom is it accountable?

- What are the services provided by the Network?

- How are these services funded and provided?

- What are the primary responsibilities of the Network?

- What is the Network's relationship with government, community, and individuals?

In the actual design of a community learning network for a specific community, other specifications will arise and be addressed in order to serve as new knowledge for the development of the functions of the system. For the purposes of this paper, only users, ownership, services and their providers, learning network responsibilities, and relationship with government, community and individuals are considered.

Users

Everyone who is a member within the community learning network is a user. The learning system is a life-long educational system. Users contribute to one another's education through the principles of complementarity and congeniality of excellences. Because of these principles, the virtues are learned and acted upon by the members.   In addition, when learners begin to take responsibility for directing their own learning and making themselves available to other learners, they control the direction of the learning endeavor.

Ownership

This leads to the next question, "Who owns the Network?"   The people own the Network.   It is a web of relationships between people and organizations and is supported by public treasuries.   Through processes of self-government, people own and manage the system and it is accountable to them.   For example, through the use of an Electronic Community Bulletin Board, classes can be offered by a teacher or created by a small group of parents.   In the case of the teacher, the necessary information is posted, such as place, time of day, class description, and syllabus.   In the case of parents, they advertise for a teacher on the Bulletin Board.

Services and Their Providers

A community learning network offers a host of learning services, from daily primary school lessons to senior citizen classes on computer word processing.   The nature of the community determines the kinds of services provided and by whom, as well as funding of such services.   Some of the service providers include:

● *At-home-learning:* Some organized learning experiences occur in the home, such as piano lessons.

● *Businesses:* Businesses in the community provide programs to learners, for example, IBM offering computer lessons at several of their retail outlets.

- ***Museums:*** Museums have long been places of learning and they continue to fulfill this role as they are more integrated into the community learning network.

- ***Science Laboratory:*** University or Corporate Laboratories play a greater role in the community learning network as they make space and time available for individuals to learn and do science.

Responsibilities of a Learning Network

The primary responsibilities of a learning network are to provide the maximum benefits to all users of the Network as well as to protect individual rights, such as protection from unscrupulous individuals. The nature of a network is its web of integrated relationships. One of the overall responsibilities of the Network is to maintain this web and integrate itself into other systems synergistically in order to be responsive to changes within the system. In addition, integration should be done in the most efficient and effective manner. Finally, the Network is responsible for safeguarding civil liberties. This can be done in cooperation with government agencies. For example, private associations can maintain Consumer Bulletins on Websites or catalogues so users and service providers know the quality of the services provided. Where private associations are unable to act in matters of civil law, government agencies interact.

Relationship with Government, Community, and Individuals

The Network is a web of relationships. In terms of providing social services to users of the system, "nodes" integrate their services with government agencies. For example, in the case of the United States Department of Education, nodes within a community learning network could integrate information services with the Department. A science CLC could provide information on and registration for various youth science programs that the Department sponsors. By integrating itself into the nodes of a community's learning network, the Department of Education is able to efficiently and effectively disseminate information and provide services.

In addition to integrating itself with government agencies, a community learning network integrates itself into the community. For example, businesses, museums, and science centers can become system nodes. As nodes, they become responsible for educational programs, curricula, and activities offered to users. A community learning network also integrates itself with individuals. The system is people, not machines or tools. Since its mission is to provide the maximum benefits to users, it creates the conditions in which individuals are able to complement their personal excellences with one another. Only in an environment that fosters growth toward achieving personal excellences is it possible for individuals to become integral beings.

Space 4: Evaluation of Core Specifications

The specifications that have been developed for the new learning network are in alignment with the mission and purposes and reflect the fundamental principles of the learning system. The users are considered to be consumers of learning as well as providers for the Greater Good of the entire learning community. In addition, the people own the system since it is they who are the Network. The system is responsible for the overall development of each member by reorganizing learning and resources around individual learners.   In addition, it is responsible for the protection of each person's civil liberties by ensuring through municipal laws and a prudent judicial system that each has equal access and opportunities to those learning resources and experiences which further self-actualization.   Furthermore, the Network integrates its functions and components into all aspects of society in order to provide users the maximum benefits of the system.

Space 2: Specifications as New Knowledge

The specifications are now part of the new knowledge necessary for developing the functions of a learning network.   They are rephrased as follows:

- All members of the community are users of a community learning network who receive its services as well as avail themselves to other learners through complementarity and congeniality of excellences in order to maximize the full benefits of the learning network.

- The members own the community's learning system and the Network is accountable to itself since the People are the Network.

- The services provided by a community learning network are dependent upon the nature of the community.

- Services in a community learning network are provided by a host of individuals and organizations within the Network.

- The primary responsibilities of the learning network are providing the maximum benefits of the Network to all users as well as safeguarding civil liberties.

- A community learning network integrates itself with government agencies, community organizations, and members of the community in order to maintain the *integrity* of the entire system.

    Finally, the process by which the specifications were developed can be recalled. Using the core definition as a guide, they were developed via an interaction between exploration and design. As a result of this exercise, the importance of *integrity* in terms of both the Network and individuals was discovered. Throughout the rest of this paper the idea of integrity will be revisited since it is important to community sustainability. After the interaction between exploration and design, the specifications were restated as a comprehensive statement (Space 3) and evaluated (Space 4) and accepted as new knowledge (Space 2).

Chapter 16: Spiral 3: Functions of a Future Learning System

The Banathy Method for designing social systems requires the functions for a future learning system to be established. Banathy suggests formulating a set of triggering questions and addressing them as part of the exercise in creating functions (1996, 138-139).

1) What are the key functions that have to be carried out?

2) How do these functions interact to constitute a system of functions?

3) What are [the] subfunctions of the key functions?

4) How do these integrate into subsystems of key functions?

5) What are the component functions of the subfunctions?

6) How can we build them into a component system of subfunctions?

What are the Key Functions of the Learning System?

The key functions are a synthesis of the mission and purposes that comprise the core definition of the learning system. In designing the functions, various aspects of the system are considered: learners and community, greater community environment, other systems, the system's members, and the system itself.

Learners and Community: One function is assisting learners with interacting with the environment in order for them to understand it better and become more apt at adjusting to its changes. A second function is supporting and training them to become self-directed learners, such as providing a variety of learning arrangements, relationships, and resources.

<u>Greater Community Environment</u>: Existing as a global learning society, national learning society, regional learning society, and local learning society is a third function of the learning system.

<u>Other Systems</u>: Integrating itself wherever and whenever possible with other systems in order to maximize the greatest benefits for individuals in their development toward self-actualization is a fourth function.

<u>Its Members</u>: Providing conditions that allow individuals to contribute to one another's learning as acts of complementary and congeniality of excellences is a fifth function. A sixth function is contributing to the Greater Good of the society.

<u>Itself</u>: Becoming an "integrated" learning system, that is, a learning network is a seventh function. An eighth function is transforming itself on a spiritual and operative level. A ninth function is governing the system through principles of self-government so that members contribute to the management of the system, allocation of its resources via free market mechanisms, protection of civil liberties, and evaluation of its services. Promoting a sustainable relationship between the political, cultural, economic, and environmental spheres of society is a final function.

According to Banathy, the functions should be presented as a model that is built on "verbs" (1996, 138).   The functions for the new learning system include:

- **Provide** a learning environment that is global, national, regional, and local in character.

- **(A1) Support** good-growth-toward-self-actualization

- **(A2) Furnish** learners with opportunities to avail themselves to other learners globally, nationally, regionally, and locally.

- **(B) Integrate** nodes of the learning system into other systems.

- **(C) Transform** the learning system spiritually and operatively.

- **(D) Manage** the learning system with principles of self-government.

- **(E) Apply** free market mechanisms to ensure efficient and effective use of resources.

- **(F) Protect** fundamental human rights.

- **(G) Balance** the political, cultural, economic, and environmental spheres with each other.

- **(H) Create** the proper learning conditions that assist individuals with recognizing the Greater Good and exploring their own paths in achieving it.

These functions interact to constitute a system of functions as illustrated in Figure 2.

Figure 2. Model of Key Functions for a Future Learning System

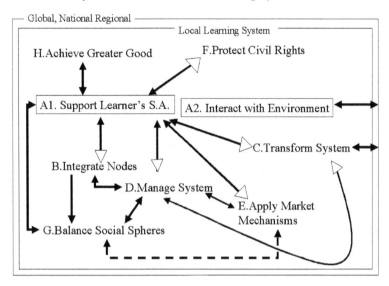

What are the Subfunctions of the Key Functions?

The process of identifying the subfunctions of a social system can continue for as long as the designers are able to deduce. However, the design of this learning system stops at the first level of subfunctions since it is not a design for a specific community, but a general framework that communities can use in designing their community learning networks.

Learning Environment Subfunctions

The learning environment function can be divided into four subfunctions: global, national, regional, and local learning networks. The key verb is "network." People and organizations within these realms are networked together. More importantly, these networks are integrated into one another to create a "meta-network," which is the learning environment (refer to Figure 3).

- <u>(Global Learning Network)</u>: **Network** organizations and communities that are involved in various international educational exchanges, cooperative enterprises, and programs.

- <u>(National Learning Network)</u>: **Network** organizations and communities that are involved in various national educational exchanges, cooperative enterprises, and programs.

- <u>(Regional Learning Network)</u>: **Network** organizations and communities that are involved in various regional educational exchanges, cooperative enterprises, and programs.

- <u>(Local Learning Network)</u>: **Network** organizations and people that are involved in various local educational exchanges, cooperative enterprises, and programs.

Figure 3. Model of Subfunctions of the Learning Environment Function

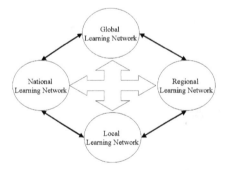

Support Learner's Self-Actualization Subfunctions

Learners are individuals who engage in learning opportunities that foster their good growth toward their own self-realization.   This occurs within a community of fellow learners, teachers, mentors, and parents.   The function of supporting self-actualization (Function A1) can be divided into eight subfunctions: self-directed learning, advising, training, mentoring, assessing, thinking, resources, and designing. These are depicted as a system of subfunctions in Figure 4 on the following page.

- (Self-directed Learning): **Establish** arrangements in which learners direct their own learning endeavors.

- (Advising): **Advise** learners of their learning options.

- (Training): **Train** learners in the necessary skills to become models of *noblesse oblige* as well as to actualize their inner potentials.

- (Mentoring or Coaching): **Facilitate** arrangements for mentoring or coaching learners.

- (Assessing): **Assist** learners with acquiring the knowledge and skills necessary for self-assessment.

- (Thinking): **Create** a learning environment that fosters a language of thinking ("terms and concepts used…to talk about thinking") as well as opportunities for learners to think (Tishman, Perkins, and Jay 1995,2-3).

- (Resources): **Make** available resources to assist learners in actualizing their inner potentials.

- (Designing): **Provide** learners with an abundance of opportunities to acquire the knowledge and skills necessary for designing social systems in a democratic self-governing society.

Figure 4. Model of Subfunctions of the Learner Function

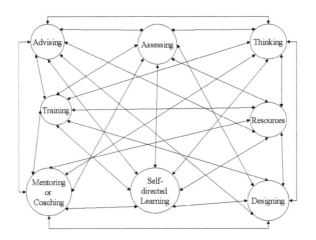

Interact with the Learning Environment Subfunctions

      When individuals interact with the learning environment (Function A2) they are in effect engaged in the activity of learning reciprocity. Learning reciprocity is supported by subfunctions that make it possible for learners to avail themselves to other learners. The system of subfunctions is illustrated in Figure 5 on the following page.

- **Establish** a matching system that matches more experienced learners with less experienced learners so that mentoring or rippling can occur.
- **Create** a monitoring system to measure the quality of learning that occurs between learners.
- **Provide** learners with the necessary resources to facilitate learning reciprocity.

Figure 5. Model of Subfunctions of the Function for Interacting with the Environment

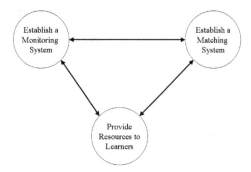

Integrate Learning Nodes Subfunction

The function for integrating learning nodes is divided into the four social spheres. Node integration as well as cross-sphere integration occurs as depicted in Figure 6 in the colored area.

- (Political Sphere [P]): **Integrate** nodes of the political sphere.

- (Cultural Sphere [C]): **Integrate** nodes of the cultural sphere.

- (Economic Sphere [Ec]): **Integrate** nodes of the economic sphere.

- (Environmental Sphere [Ev]): **Integrate** nodes of the environmental sphere.

- (Cross-Sphere Integration [black area]): **Cross-Integrate** nodes between spheres.

Figure 6. Model of Subfunctions of the Function for Integrating Nodes

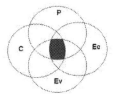

Transform Learning System Subfunctions

The function of transforming the learning system is made possible when feedback within the local learning system is provided to the transformational function and when the transformational function receives input from the greater learning environment.   Recall that transformation is the re-design of the entire system.   Figure 7 illustrates how these subfunctions are arranged into a system of subfunctions.

- **Provide** opportunities for learners to learn in accordance with the laws of nature at each stage of life.
- **Incorporate** into the learning experience opportunities to learn and understand future trends.
- **Create** for learners learning arrangements that allow them to develop and understand multiple perspectives.

Figure 7. Model of Subfunctions of the Transformative Learning Function

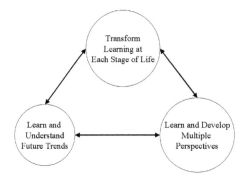

Manage the Learning System Subfunctions

In order to manage the local learning system, it is necessary to establish the management function upon a set of principles of self-government.   These principles are restated as a set of management subfunctions such as the ones illustrated in Figure 8.

(First Principle):

● **Create** self-governing systems.

(Second Principle):

● **Establish** education resource centers.

(Third Principle):

● **Create** a just tax system.

(Fourth Principle):

● **Maintain** sustainability between social spheres.

Figure 8. Model of Subfunctions of the Management Function

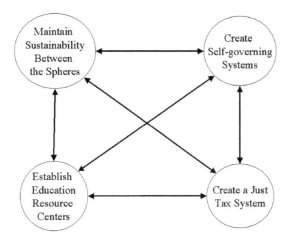

Apply Free Market Mechanisms Subfunctions

Applying free market mechanisms is one way to support the process of self-actualization. Commensurable goods and utilities are more efficiently and effectively distributed by a free market than by a centralized system. The subfunctions are rephrased as statements of horizontal equity, government, and civil society. These are arranged into a system of subfunctions as illustrated in Figure 9.

(Horizontal Equity):

- **Ensure** that horizontal equity (equal payment) exists between taxpayers for public services.

- **Ensure** that horizontal equity (equal access) exists between users of public services.

(Government)

- **Reduce** the federal government's role wherever state or local government can act more efficiently and effectively.

(Civil Society)

- **Encourage** private and civil associations to provide for social services wherever and whenever possible.

- **Encourage** the development of a sustainable economic sphere.

Figure 9. Model of Subfunctions of the Free Market Function

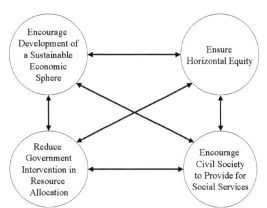

Protect Civil Liberties Subfunctions

Protecting civil liberties is an important function in the learning network and requires subfunctions within the political and cultural spheres. The purpose of the State is to establish laws that protect the basic human rights recognized by civilized society. Furthermore, it creates agencies that enforce such laws. Civil society ensures the protection of proportional productive and recipient equality[1] through the voluntary participation of private organizations and individuals. These ideas are rephrased as subfunctions below and illustrated in Figure 10.

- **Establish** a system of government that makes laws protecting civil rights.

- **Establish** a system of government that enforces the law.

- **Establish** within the cultural sphere private organizations that monitor proportional productive and recipient equality.

---

[1] Norton defines proportional productive equality as equality that "obtains when A and B are alike doing the work for which each is by nature best suited." Proportional recipient equality "obtains when A and B alike possess the particular goods and utilities to which each is entitled" (1991, 161).

Figure 10. Model of Subfunctions of the Civil Liberties Function

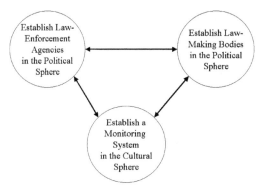

Balance Social Spheres Subfunctions

Balancing the social spheres is an important function in the learning network and is achieved through a variety of subfunctions. These are arranged into a system of subfunctions as depicted in Figure 11.

- **Establish** a system for integrating systems.

- **Create** capacities for transformation.

- **Establish** a sustainability monitoring system.

Figure 11. Model of Subfunctions of the Sustainability Function

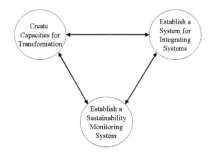

Achieve Greater Good Subfunctions

The Greater Good is an end as well as a means of the learning system.   It is achieved through at least two subfunctions and these are illustrated in Figure 12.

● **Provide** an organic learning environment in which the virtues are fostered in individuals.

● **Provide** opportunities for learners to act on the virtues.

Figure 12. Model of Subfunctions of the Function for Achieving the Greater Good

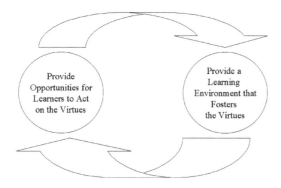

Space 4: Evaluation of Functions

The functions and subfunctions necessary for a future public community learning network have been designed.   Since the task of the design is to create a generalized framework that can be used by many communities, a detailed analysis of the subfunctions is not addressed.   These are only considered in the design of a learning network that reflects the character of a specific community.

Based upon this contingency, the functions have synthesized the mission and purposes.   The basic principles of self-actualization, brain-compatible learning, symbolic interactionist social psychology, self-government, learner-centered and learner-directed education, and systemic design are recognizable in the functions and subfunctions of the learning system.   Furthermore, the functions necessary to provide for the synergistic relationships between these principles have been provided.

Space 2: Functions as New Knowledge

The functions that were developed in the design solution space (Space 3) have been evaluated (Space 4) and now serve as new knowledge (Space 2) for the creation of the enabling systems.

Chapter 17: Spiral 4: Enabling Systems

Chapter 16 addressed the "functions" of the learning system. In this chapter "form" is discussed. The design of the enabling systems involves two questions: 1) What are the elements that have the capacity and capability to carry out the functions? 2) How are these elements arranged in order to carry out the functions? These questions are considered using Banathy's method for creating the Management and Organization Systems. The systems are developed in respect to the four social spheres. This is a unique aspect of this treatise since it offers a different perspective from that of Banathy's "Learning Society" or Reigeluth's "Third-Wave Educational System." After discussing the Management and Organization Systems, the Systemic Environment (Implementation) System is presented. It is the larger system in which the learning system is embedded, that is, the strategies that are used to gather people together to discuss, plan, and implement the new learning system.

Banathy refers to the Management System as "The first NOUN-BASED model that...will have the organizational capacity and staff capability to guide the educational system and ensure that the functions will be carried out as specified in the functions model" (1991, 188-189). The questions that are addressed in developing this model include (Banathy 1996, 140):

1. What design will enable the system to select the processes that "transform" the functions into ongoing actions?
2. What design will enable the system to conceive and plan the initiation of those actions?

3. What design will enable the system to motivate and energize the individual and collective action of those who carry out the processes?

4. What design will enable the system to work with the environment in order to collect and analyze information that is of value to the system and that enhances the accomplishment of functions?

5. What design will enable the system to work with the environment in order to acquire and manage the resources that are needed by the system?

6. What design will enable the system to identify actual and potential problems, threats and opportunities?

7. What design will enable the system to engage the system in continuous organizational learning and nurture design capacity?

The second NOUN-BASED model is the ORGANIZATION MODEL. It is the modeling of "a system which will have the organizational capacity and the staff capability to carry out the functions as specified in the functions model" (ibid., 189). The questions that are considered in developing this model are (ibid., 189-190):

1. What organizational and personal capabilities are required to carry out the identified functions?

2. What system components and people will have those capacities and capabilities?

3. How should we organize the selected components in relational (vertical/horizontal) arrangements?

4. What authority/responsibility should be assigned to whom?

5. What resources should be allocated to what component?

The Systemic Environment (Implementation) System embeds the Management and Organization Systems.   This addresses the techniques used to implement the future learning system.

Management System

The components that implement the functions and subfunctions of the learning system are listed in the following manner.

- *Local Community Learning Network Administrative Office (CLNAO)*: Replaces the local school board structure and serves as the main political component for developing and maintaining the learning network.   It funds chartered learning pods and community learning centers.

- *Individualized Curricular Development Office (ICDO)*: Serves as the political component for diagnosing and advising learners as well as assisting them with developing curricula and matching them with other learners in the Network.   Each ICDO is established by the CLNAO within walking distance to people's homes.

- *Learning Pod*: Serves as the cultural vehicle for facilitating a learner's curricular program.   It is a private group of learners and professional and/or lay-teachers that receives a charter from the CLNAO.

- *Community Learning Center (CLC)*: Replaces the school and serves as a cultural component that develops and provides educational services and resources for learners.   It is a public or private entity that is staffed with professional and/or lay-teachers who work with learning pods in developing individualized curricula for learners.   It receives a charter from the CLNAO.

- *Professional Teacher*: An individual recognized by the CLNAO who has acquired knowledge of human growth and development and educational pedagogy through formal training, personal study, and/or experience, who has demonstrated capacity to guide the learning activities of others, and who is primarily responsible for an individual's learning program in the public learning network.

- *Lay-Teacher*: Recognized by the CLNAO as a person who knows or does something so well that she can teach it to another person in the public learning network.

- *Advisor*: Recognized by the CLNAO as a professional teacher who works within the ICDO to diagnose and advise learners.

- *University*: Serves as a cultural component for preparing people to become educators, scholars, and free thinkers in an environment of "higher education."

- *Inter-University Futures Collaborative*: Serves as a cultural component for the Network. It is a group of university learning centers that operates within an individualized curricular context with an emphasis on future trends.

- *Community College*: A public institution of higher learning that offers credited or non-credited courses in vocations and avocations.

- *Futures Institute*: Serves as a cultural component within a community college system that assists communities in developing "capacities for transformation."

- *Knowledge Democracy Network*: Serves as a political component that creates a network of neighborhood leaders who broaden the involvement and interest of local citizens in local self-governance.

- *Trade School*: Serves as a cultural component for providing knowledge and skills within a trade and is networked with business organizations.

- *Centers for Learning*: Serve as the cultural components for learning and include but not limited to CLCs, learning pods, universities, and trade schools.

- *Apprenticeship or Internship*: Serves as an economic component for assisting learners in acquiring the knowledge and developing the skills and dispositions of one's chosen trade.

- *Businesses*: Serve as sustainable economic entities within the economic sphere that create and sell products or services directly to members of the community.   They work with the learning system by availing themselves to the learning network.

- *Local Environmental Organization*: A private organization that is concerned about environmental sustainability.   It serves as an environmental component that assists the learning network with creating an environmentally sustainable learning system.

- *Farms, National Parks, and the Greater Environs*: Serve as cultural, economic, or environmental components in the learning network.   As learning resources, they assist learners with connecting with nature.

- *Natural Systems*: Serve as environmental components that help learners to understand systems within the environmental sphere.

- *Designed Systems*: Serve as environmental components that employ technology and knowledge so that the natural systems may be self-governing.

- *Private and Civil Associations*: Serve as cultural components that provide resources to learners and help monitor the learning system.

- *Centers of Worship*: Serve as cultural components that provide a parochial foundation in virtuous acts and achieving the Greater Good.

- *Educational Foundations*: Private foundations that fund system components such as CLCs and learning pods.

- *Board of Directors*: Serves as a political component that represents the interests of the community in directing the affairs of the CLNAO.

- *Legislative Bodies*: Serve as political components that bring people together in assembly to decide on issues.

- *Legislative Branch*: Serves as a political component that represents the interests of the community through elected representatives who serve in general assembly and decide on issues that regulate the CLNAO and provide public funds to support the Network.

- *Executive Branch*: Serves as a political component to assist the CLNAO Board of Directors with municipal issues. It is the municipal executive branch, such as a mayor or county executive.

- *Judicial Branch*: Serves as a political component that makes rulings on municipal cases affecting the learning system.

- *Law-Enforcement Agency*: Serves as a political component that enforces legislation.

- *Public Voucher System*: Serves as a political instrument for monitoring the usage of public resources. It assists the CLNAO with adequately funding chartered CLCs and learning pods.

- *Public Audit System*: Serves as a political instrument for determining if each public chartered entity is successfully meeting its goals and objectives and using resources in accordance with established public guidelines and criteria.

- *Integration Component*: Serves as the component within each sphere to assist with integrating functions and components into other spheres.

- *Monitoring Component*: Serves as the component within each sphere to assist with monitoring those activities that directly or indirectly affect other spheres.

The Organization

In this section the characteristics of the organizational elements and people working in the learning system are identified.   In addition, the organizational relationships of the elements identified in the Management System are addressed and their models presented in terms of the four spheres of society.

Characteristics

The bedrock of the future learning system is self-actualization and sustainability.   The organizational elements and persons working in the learning system should embody the following characteristics:

Organizational Characteristics

- *Learning Community:* Each organizational element should be a system whose members act as a learning community.   Fred Kofman and Peter Senge identify three foundations that are essential for learning communities: "(1) a culture based on transcendent human values of love, wonder, humility, and compassion; (2) a set of practices for generative conversation and coordinated action; and (3) a capacity to see and work with the flow of life as a system" (1995, 32).

- *Self-Governing:* Each organizational element should be a system whose members act upon principles of self-government.

- *Self-actualizing:* Each organizational element should be a system whose members embody the qualities of *noblesse oblige* and promote the Greater Good.

Human Characteristics

The human characteristics that should be embodied by mature individuals working in the learning network to produce and maintain a self-realizing society and to guide others toward their self-realization include those that Abraham Maslow lists for self-actualizing individuals (Maslow 1987, 128-143).

- *Clear Perception of Reality:* Each individual should be able to perceive more clearly what *is* the real world and to look beyond those anthropocentric elements that people confuse with the real world. In other words, the ability to "detect the spurious, the fake, and the dishonest personality, and in general to judge people correctly and efficiently" (ibid., 128).

- *Acceptance:* Each individual should be able to be content with who he is. He accepts himself at all levels: love, safety, belongingness, honor, and self-respect.

- *Spontaneity:* Each individual should be able to be spontaneous in outer life through the activities with which he engages and in inner life through his thoughts and ideas and not to allow convention to supplant this spontaneity.

- *Problem Centering:* Each individual should be able to see the world beyond his own ego. He is able to connect himself with a mission far greater than his own existence. Most importantly, in accepting this mission and actualizing it, he constantly explores the basic issues and eternal questions of humanity that are referred to as philosophical or ethical.

- *Solitude:* Each individual should be able to enjoy periods of solitude so as to reflect upon life and become more self-disciplined and responsible.

- *Autonomy:* Each individual should be able to act autonomously—to be self-deciding, self-governing, pro-active, responsible, and self-disciplined.

- *Fresh Appreciation:* Each individual should be able to appreciate the basic goods of life.

- *Peak Experiences:* Each individual should be able to experience certain moments in which there is a sense of transcendence of life.

- *Human Kinship:* Each individual should be able to have a sincere kinship with other human beings despite cultural, national, or racial differences.

- *Humility and Respect:* Each individual should be "democratic" in the way he interacts with other individuals, that is, friendly with anyone who is of suitable character despite the other's class, education, political belief, race, or color. Furthermore, each should be able to develop the mental disposition that one can learn from others.

- *Interpersonal Relationships:* Each individual should be able to have a great capacity to love and transcend the boundaries of the ego.

- *Ethics:* Each individual should be able to live an integrated life and have a profound sense of right and wrong grounded in an ethics for the common good.

- *Means and Ends:* Each individual should be able to distinguish between means and ends, that is to be able to determine for himself the good life within an ethical framework that defines the means that are commensurate with his ends; and to appreciate the means as a self-actualizing activity.

- *Humor:* Each individual should be able to possess a sense of humor.

- *Creativity:* Each individual should be able to act creatively in his work.

- ***Question, Analyze, and Evaluate Enculturation:*** Each individual should be able to question, analyze, and evaluate enculturation, but still be able to maintain an attachment with one's culture.

- ***Imperfections:*** Each individual should be able to accept the reality that he is not perfect.

- ***Values:*** Each individual should be able to adhere to a value system that accepts the nature of the self, human nature, the nature of social life, and the nature of the natural world and physical universe.

- ***Resolution of Dichotomies:*** Each individual should be able to resolve dichotomies, such as heart and head, reason and instinct, cognition and conation, work and play.

Organizational Relationships

Another question that should be addressed is, "How should the selected components be organized in relational arrangements?" The following figures assist in understanding the relationships between the components.

Figure 13. Structural Arrangements for the Future Learning System

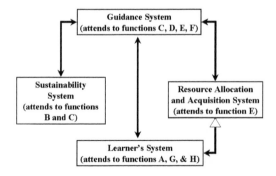

Using Banathy's Map of Structural Arrangements (1992, 90), a general model of the component arrangements is depicted in Figure 13.   The Learner's System is at the center of the model since all other components are arranged around him.   A resource allocation and acquisition system exists in order for the learner to have and use those goods and utilities that further his self-actualization.   A guidance system helps him with developing his individualized curriculum as well as with accounting for the use of resources in the system.   A sustainability system exists in order to ensure that the system is operating in synergy with the four social spheres.   A more detailed description of these components in relationship to the four social spheres is provided in Figures 14—18.

Figure 14. Relational Arrangements Between the Four Spheres of Society

Figure 14 depicts the horizontal relationship between the four spheres of society, political sphere (P), cultural sphere (C), economic sphere (Ec), and environmental sphere (Ev).   The colored area represents the interaction between them. Figures 15—22 illustrate the component arrangements within each sphere and their relationships with one another in the learning system.

Figure 15. Relational Arrangements Between The Political Sphere Components

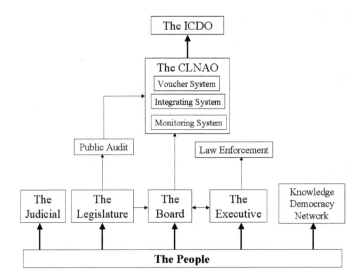

People are the foundation for any democratic political system. In this learning system several components exist to implement the political functions of the Network. The Knowledge Democracy Network exists to create self-democratic neighborhood networks within the learning community to assist in fostering participatory self-government.

The Executive Branch of government refers to the mayor or county executive. It works with the CLNAO Board of Directors regarding municipal issues, such as setting up a public transformation system between CLCs or cooperating with other government agencies in enforcing law.

The CLNAO Board of Directors is elected directly by the people. It interprets law passed by the municipal legislature and employs those individuals required to implement the law, such as administrators. Furthermore, it allocates public funds to the CLNAO administrators for educational programs such as CLC development.

The Legislative Branch of government is the municipal legislature. It passes laws and regulations regarding the learning community as well as funds the CLNAO. Furthermore, it employs outside auditors to audit all parties that receive public funds for use in the learning system.

The Judicial Branch hears civil cases pertaining to the community learning network as well as makes rulings regarding law established by the Legislature.

The CLNAO is the primary political component for implementing the political functions of the learning network. It is staffed with administrators who in turn hire the necessary individuals for implementing particular aspects of the CLNAO's mission.

The ICDO is a neighborhood branch office of the CLNAO that is primarily responsible for learner diagnosis and advisement, learner-to-learner matching, and individualized curricular development. The primary administrators of an ICDO are professional teachers.

Figure 16. Relational Arrangements Between The Cultural Sphere Components

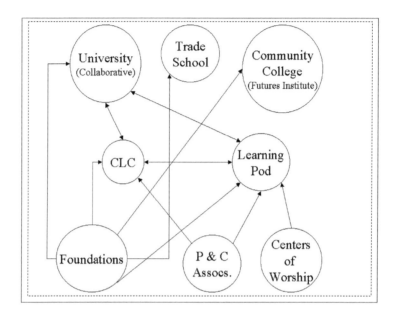

Figure 16 depicts the systemic relational arrangements between the cultural sphere components.   The outer-solid line represents the Greater Environs and includes those components such as farms and parks.   The outer-dotted line represents people. People permeate the entire sphere and all components are encompassed within the framework of mature people.   Furthermore, each entity is illustrated as circles in order to represent the horizontal relationships between the components.

Educational foundations in the community help finance the learning network. They are one source of funding for CLCs, learning pods, universities, community colleges, and trade schools.

The CLC is a private or public entity that develops and provides educational services and resources. It is staffed with professional and lay-teachers. Professional teachers come from teacher colleges within universities. Lay-teachers, such as parents, come from the greater community.

The learning pod is a private entity for facilitating a learner's curricular program. It is staffed with professional and lay-teachers. As with the CLC, professional teachers come from the university and lay-teachers come from the greater community. The learning pod, in cooperation with parents, the ICDO, and CLCs, assists learners with developing individualized curricula. It is networked with various elements, such as professional associations, centers of worship, and universities.

Private and Civil Associations, such as professional associations for teachers, parent associations, children's associations, and parent-teacher associations, support the endeavors of members in the learning system.

The university is a private or public entity. Graduates from teacher colleges or current students of teacher colleges serve the system as teachers or apprentice-teachers. It also serves the system by providing it with the most current research on theory, methodology, and application.

The Inter-University Futures Collaborative is an extension of the university and falls within its realm. Though the focus is on the future, it is part of the university system and contributes to the teaching endeavor by working in partnership with

Colleges of Education, CLCs, and learning pods (refer to Appendix).

The trade school is a private entity that is supported by educational foundations. Firms and businesses establish most of these foundations through professional business associations such as the Chamber of Commerce or Trade Guild.

The Community College contributes to the learning network by offering credited or non-credited courses in vocations or avocations. The Futures Institute is part of the community college system and contributes to the learning network through course offerings, seminars, and projects on "capacities for transformation."

Centers of worship contribute to the educational endeavor of the learning system by availing themselves to learners. For example, a Catholic parish could advertise through the CLNAO its various learning pods. Though these pods are sectarian and not entitled to public funds, they are still entitled to public resources, such as CLCs, libraries, and museums. The vouchers used by the members of these pods account for the utilization of public facilities. For example, when a learner from a Catholic pod goes to a public museum for an educational program, that voucher card accounts for the expense incurred by the public for providing a service. The museum records in its voucher system that Student A from Catholic Pod B attended Program XYZ on December 1ˢᵗ. The voucher card records that on December 1ˢᵗ Program XYZ was attended at Museum ABC. The Learning Pod-CLC arrangement promotes the democratic principle of separation of church and state as well as the principles of self-actualization.

Finally, though not illustrated in Figure 16, there are integration and monitoring components in the learning system. Each entity decides the development and employment issues in relation to the learning system.

Figure 17. Relational Arrangements Between The Economic Sphere Components

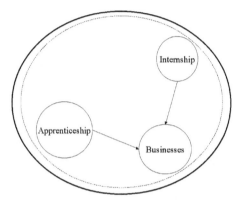

Like the cultural sphere, the economic components are illustrated as circles in order to demonstrate their horizontal relationship. Furthermore, the outer-dotted line represents the "sphere of people" since it is they who facilitate the functions of the economic sphere. Also, it is they who manage the sphere. The outer-solid line depicts the greater environment.

The apprenticeship is a formalized learning relationship with a master in a particular trade that is acknowledged by a legal contract between the apprentice and the guild or firm to which the master belongs. The master teaches the apprentice the knowledge and skills necessary for learning the trade as he passes through a series of learning stages to achieve the status of master (Gardner 1999, 31).

The internship, unlike an apprenticeship, is informal supervised training for a learner within a trade.   It is a short-term commitment by the learner to the interning party so that he gains practical experience in his trade.

Figure 18. Relational Arrangements Between the Environmental Sphere Components

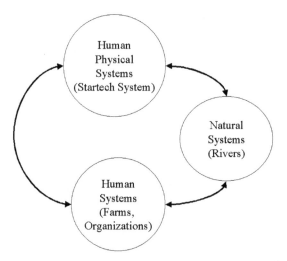

The environmental sphere consists of three types of systems: natural systems, human systems, and human physical systems.   These systems are depicted as circles in order to demonstrate their horizontal relationships.   Natural systems are those systems that nature has organized, such as rivers, forests, lakes, mountains, and fields.   Human systems are those systems that have integrated themselves into natural systems, such as farms.   Human physical systems are man-made systems that help humanity to live in harmony with natural systems.   The Startech Waste-to-Energy System is one example. It is a waste converter system that transforms waste into plasma converted gas (PCG) and the PCG in turn is converted into hydrogen for clean and safe energy.

Within each of these systems exists the integration and monitoring systems. Nature reacts to any imbalances in the natural system.   Human systems are designed to monitor the synergistic relationship between themselves and the environment.   Human physical systems, such as the Startech System, are designed to be integrative.   They are also designed to assist people with monitoring them and fixing or replacing their parts.

Implementation System

The final enabling system is the Implementation System (Banathy's Systemic Environment System).   It embeds the system that is designed, which in this case is the learning system (Banathy 1996, 141).   Several techniques exist for communities to design a learning system.   The technique subscribed to in this treatise is an adaptation of the Communities of the Future (COTF) model for Building Capacities for Transformation.   Rick Smyre in, *Building Capacities for Community Transformation*, defines transformation as "the type of change that restructures the very nature of what has existed before" (2000, 13).   The capacities that COTF believes are required to transform a community include 1) a community based electronic infrastructure, 2) developing a futures context, 3) process leadership, 4) twenty-first century concept of the common good, and 5) basic skills for the twenty-first century, such as ability to access the Internet, facilitate small groups of diverse people, and help people connect and view things from a different perspective (ibid., 14-16).

Building capacities for transformation occurs through processes of dialogue and planning, which Smyre refers to as parallel processes.   Parallel processes is "doing" and "thinking" simultaneously.   Strategic planning is the "doing," the setting of goals, objectives and benchmarks and then achieving them.   Generative dialogue is the "thinking," the gathering of people to talk about ideas.

The Implementation scheme that I have developed includes the following steps for communities to design and implement a learning system: generate dialogue on transformation, learn about transformational learning and learning networks, create a new learning system, present the framework to the community, and implement it using a democratic process of decision-making.   One important point about implementation is that the system first designed may not be the final system agreed upon by the entire community.   Implementation occurs through iterative cycles in which plans change as new ideas or concepts are developed.   Finally, the process is not something that happens quickly.   Some members will experience frustration with systemic design because it takes time and requires them to overcome their misconceptions.

Generating Dialogue on Transformation

1.   Create a discussion group (learning node) of ten to fifteen people who are interested in the idea of transformation.   The facilitator of the group should provide a list of reading materials on new realities and future trends.   The group should meet once a month or every two months to report their findings.

2.   Once the group feels that they have a grasp of the idea of transformation, they should begin to include more people in the learning node.

3.   This new group should break into separate learning nodes of ten to fifteen people per node with one original member of the first node acting as a Node Facilitator.

4.   Each Node Facilitator should repeat "Step 1."

5. All nodes should eventually report back into a General Assembly. The first meeting should focus on thinking about issues from a futures perspective. A list of issues that could be thought of from a futures perspective is generated.

6. Each node should look at a particular issue and try to resolve that issue from a futures context.

7. Finally, each node should report back into a General Assembly. Representatives from each node should give a presentation on their Issue—a) What is the issue? b) What was the future context? c) How did you resolve it? A time for questions-and-answers should be allotted after each presentation.

Learning about Transformational Learning and Learning Networks

1. As a General Assembly, the members learn about transformational learning and learning networks. Members should become familiar with the literature on the principles of self-actualization, brain-compatible learning, symbolic interactionist social psychology, self-government, learner-centered/learner-directed education, and systemic design. Someone with in-depth knowledge on these issues should facilitate the learning in order to guide the members throughout the learning process. This person could be referred to as a Learning Facilitator.

2. The General Assembly should break into its learning nodes to research the above principles. Each node should be assigned only one principle. The Node Facilitators guide the learning within each of their nodes and are supported by the Learning Facilitator.

3. Each month the General Assembly gathers to listen to a presentation by one of the nodes on the principle it researched. Each presentation should be supplemented by

a hardcopy to be given to the audience. A time for questions-and-answers should be allotted at the end of each presentation.

Creating a New Learning System

1. After the nodes have given their presentations and the entire group feels comfortable with the new knowledge and ideas, the General Assembly breaks into its nodes to address the question, "What kind of learning system do we create that is in alignment with the new knowledge and ideas?" This is only a brainstorming session and short phrases should be generated.

2. After each node has generated a list of ideas or short phrases, the nodes should gather in General Assembly to select the ideas. Since over a hundred ideas can be generated, Banathy suggests using organizational software such as CogniScope Software (1996, 149-151). A selection committee of about one-third of the assembly should be created to select the top five ideas.

3. After the top five ideas have been chosen, the next question for each node to address is: "How do we create a learning network?" This, too, is only a brainstorming session and short phrases should be generated.

4. Repeat Step 2. The selection committee decides if the "what's" are commensurate with the "how's."

5. The group creates an Action Framework to address the "why," "what," how," "when," and "where" of implementing the ideas. This framework should be brought forward to the greater community.

Presenting the Framework to the Community

1. The framework should be presented to the community via a variety of media, especially the Internet. The group should also present the framework at forums and town meetings so that the community understands it and can have their questions answered. Another idea is to present the framework in increments to the community.

2. Work with community colleges to create Future Institutes and universities to create Inter-University Futures Collaboratives to take the lead in the educational transformation by serving as "think tanks" for the community.

3. Have a group of people work with the community in providing them information for their own thinking transformation, such as the creation of neighborhood learning webs, small groups of people in a neighborhood who become familiar with the ideas of transformation. Another idea is to create a website that includes discussion groups, bibliographies for worthwhile reading, and links to other community websites that address community transformation.

4. Encourage people to network with other communities in order to "build as many common capacity building projects between the two areas as possible" (Smyre 2000, 21).

5. Smyre suggests involving the local chamber of commerce in order to establish a "process leadership" development process. It is rooted in three core values: "1) understanding the impact of future trends, 2) building multiple processes of connections, thinking and decision making, and 3) evolving personal attributes capable of 21ˢᵗ century leadership" (ibid.). People within the Chamber should begin to think of ways to develop a digital economy within their community.

6. Create a group that will establish an electronic community network, such as the Blacksburg Electronic Village that Virginia Polytechnic has created for the community of Blacksburg, Virginia.

7. Establish a Knowledge Democracy project in several neighborhoods that assists people with understanding and practicing direct consensus democracy.

8. Make it a community commitment that all households in each neighborhood have at least one computer so they will be connected with one another electronically (ibid., 22).

9. **Implement the Framework** using a democratic system of decision-making.

Space 4: Evaluation of the Enabling System

The most general components of a public community learning network necessary for implementing the functions have been established within each social sphere. In addition, the relational arrangements between each of them have been described. The monitoring and integrating systems of the components have been provided and their arrangements and relationships explained. Furthermore, a description of the organizational and personal capabilities has been given that is in accordance with the principles of self-actualization and self-government. In terms of organizations, this includes at least the ability to be a learning community and a self-governing, self-actualizing organization. The personal characteristics necessary for mature people working in the Network include at least those that Abraham Maslow identifies in self-actualizing individuals.

Finally, the implementation system was provided to assist communities with designing and implementing a new learning system. In order to create a learning network, capacities to transform are required. These capacities include the development of a community-based electronic infrastructure, a futures context, process leadership, a community concept of the common good, and basic skills necessary for life in the twenty-first century.

Space 2: Enabling Systems as New Knowledge

The enabling systems designed in the design solution space (Space 3) have been evaluated (Space 4) and now serve as the new knowledge space (Space 2) for the development of the three models of the learning system presented in Chapter 18: systems-environment model, functions/structure model, and the process-behavioral model.

Chapter 18: Space 5: Model of a Future Learning System and Its Environment

In this chapter a future learning system and its environment are observed through three different lenses, a bird's eye-view, still picture view, and a motion picture view. The bird's eye-view is a systems-environment model. It is a general description of the system that helps define the rules that guide systems-environment relationships, interactions, and mutual interdependence (Banathy 1992, 22).

The still picture lens is a functions/structure model. It enables designers to describe the system's goals, identify the functions that attain the goals and purposes, specify the relationships of those functions, define elements that activate and manage the functions, and describe the organizational relationships of the elements (ibid.). Hence, it is a recapitulation of the functions and enabling systems that have been established in Chapters 16 and 17. For the purposes of this paper, only reference is made to the functions and enabling systems since the models are already available in "still picture" form in the previous chapters.

The motion picture lens is a process model since it looks at what the system does throughout time and how it functions. More specifically, the model describes the following about the system (ibid., 22-23):

- receives, screens/assesses, and processes input,
- transforms input for use in the system,

- engages in operations that attend to the purpose(s) and goals of the system and produce the expected outcomes,

- continuously assesses and guides the transformation operations,

- processes the outcomes and assesses their adequacy, and

- makes adjustments and changes in the system and, if indicated, transforms the system based on the assessment as well as information (feedback) coming from the environment.

Systems-Environment Model

Figure 19 portrays a general systems-environment model (ibid., 34, 40). It illustrates the societal aspects of the system (the general environment and the systemic environment), the system boundary, breaks within the boundaries, inputs and outputs, and mechanisms for transformation and feedback. Recall that the white-tipped arrow is feedback and the black-tipped arrow is feedforward. Figure 20 illustrates the concept of embeddedness. Since the learning system in this paper is developed within the four spheres of society, Banathy's model of embeddedness is adapted. What Banathy refers to as The Overall Societal Environment, Geopolitical Environment, and Systemic Environment, I refer to as the four social spheres. This is elaborated upon later in the paper.

Figure 19. Banathy's Systems-Environment Model (ibid., 34)

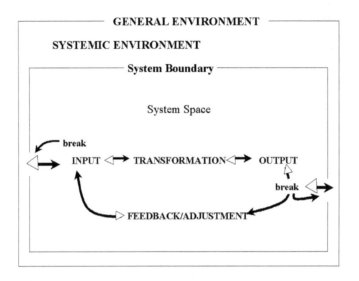

Figure 20. Embeddedness of a Future Learning System

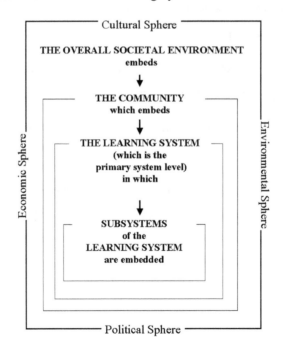

The Learning System In Its Environment

<u>Space and Time</u>

Learning systems exist in space and time and within space and time they change, that is, they grow, decline, or develop.   Time refers to the past, present, and future. Since the future learning system is for a self-actualizing society, parents, teachers, mentors, and advisors should assist learners in applying the Principle of the Act.   The Principle of the Act as established by John Dewey, George Herbert Mead, and other symbolic interactionists holds that a commensurable act of an individual is one that is commensurate with the individual throughout time.   Thus, the act I did a while ago should be commensurate with the act I do now which should be commensurate with the act I do next.   This is what Norton refers to as a state of *eudaimonia*.   The act that I did yesterday is an act that helps me to actualize my potential today which in turn helps me to actualize my potential tomorrow.   This is why Dewey stresses that learning activities should be commensurate with each other.   They should not only add to the knowledge and skills base of the learner but also contribute to whom he is to be.

<u>Growth, Decline, and Development</u>

Other concepts that characterize the learning system and its relationship with the environment are growth, decline, and development.   Banathy defines growth as change in size or quantity, decline as decline in quality that may lead to termination of the system, and development as a purposeful increase in quality (ibid., 36).   Development is measured by addressing at least four basic questions that should yield a "Yes" answer to each.   These questions relate to the system at the individual level, learning system level, and the societal level respectfully:

1. **(Individual Level)** Are people actualizing their potentials, i.e. becoming who they are?

2. **(Learning System Level)** Is self-actualization occurring in a democratic, republican framework in which the principles of self-government are being actualized?

3. **(Societal Level)** Does sustainability exist between the four spheres of society? Is the learning system contributing to the evolutionary progress of humanity?

Embeddedness

As has been previously asserted, the learning system is embedded within the four spheres of society that Banathy refers to as the general environment and which I call the overall societal environment. Banathy describes the general environment as "all things that surround the system, and it includes everything that may affect the system or that may be affected by the system" (1992, 28). It is community that expands from the immediate local community outward toward the global community (ibid., 37). It is those world realities and their implications that are stated in Part 3 with which the system must contend in order to survive.

Within the overall societal environment are the global, federal, national, state and municipal levels of government that influence and are influenced by the learning system. Some of the relationships between the overall societal environment and the local learning system are identified on the following pages.

At the global level, organizations such as UNESCO assist in facilitating cultural exchanges or creating a global learning network. Other international organizations help teachers to keep abreast of new developments, network with other teachers, and support research in learning and human development. Human rights organizations influence civil rights in local learning systems. In societies that give little credence to human rights, these organizations play a vital role in assisting them to identify with universal human rights and incorporate them into their learning systems. Religious organizations, such as the Roman Catholic Church, assist members of a local learning network with achieving the Greater Good. Through a network of relations and internal systems, Catholics within the local community learning network can have access to other Catholics across the globe. Though both do not occupy the same physical geographical location, both are alike in loving the Greater Good but qualitatively different in the way the Good is achieved.

At the federal level the government plays an important role in protecting civil rights. In the case of the United States, a Bill of Rights exists to protect freedoms of speech and assembly. To ensure that these rights are protected, Americans have established a justice system that hears cases regarding violations of these rights. Besides the legal arena, the federal government assists the community learning network with supporting learners' self-actualization. The main component for this interaction is The Department of Education. The Department of Education could do many things, such as disseminate information to state agencies or local learning systems, provide teaching workshops for professional teachers, or issue grants to local learning systems for the development of transformational learning networks. However, the one thing that the federal government should not do, as it is doing today, is set national learning standards or benchmarks for all learning systems to meet. This action violates principles such as self-actualization, brain-compatible learning, and self-government.

At the national level several private and civil associations assist local learning systems with supporting learners' self-actualization. These could include associations for creating better communication between teachers and parents such as a national Parent-Teacher Association. A PTA also helps a community in achieving the common good by making parents and teachers aware of the different values and beliefs in the community and to create opportunities for community dialogue.

Similar to the federal government, the state too plays an important role in protecting civil liberties. In addition to those rights identified in the Bill of Rights, citizens have individual state rights. Each state has a judicial system for hearing cases that pertain to state rights. Each state should also have agencies that interact with local learning systems in order to create a more efficient and effective "meta-learning system." One way for a state to interact with a local learning system is to integrate its state functions into the functions of the learning system. For example, the CLNAO and ICDO could assist the State Department of Education in disseminating information and providing state services. The State Department of Education could also assist a local learning system with transforming itself and integrating its nodes within other local learning systems in the meta-network. This could be done via a state university, such as Virginia Technical University's Blacksburg Electronic Village.

At the municipal level the legislature, executive, and judicial are responsible for creating and maintaining a safe and efficient public learning environment that supports learners' self-actualization.   In addition to protecting individual civil liberties, the municipality is directly responsible for funding the network.   The municipal legislature provides funds to the CLNAO to create the public learning system.   This includes the voucher system, grants, facilities, electronic bulletin board, etc.   Also at the municipal level, other components assist the learning system in becoming a transformational learning system.   Religious or spiritual organizations help individuals with achieving the Greater Good.   Local market mechanisms assist with the allocation of resources. Inter-University Futures Collaboratives monitor community sustainability and cooperate with other components to maintain it.   Hence, in a model society, all systems within the municipal sphere are transformational learning systems.

Embedded within the societal environment is the specific community. According to Banathy, the community "has a direct and ongoing influence on" the learning system "and is connected with it by high intensity interactions" (ibid., 38). In alignment with the principles of self-actualization and self-government, he describes learners as people who have learned "how to realize their potential, how to make valuable contributions to the community and the society, and how to become competent and participating citizens" (ibid.).

It is very difficult to draw a line between the community and the learning system since the community is part of the learning system.   Despite this apparent difficulty of distinction, community is part of the societal environment because it is not under the control of the learning system but the learning system is under the control of the community.   Control rests in the hands of the people.   The people through voluntary association and participatory democratic actions create a public learning system that is in alignment with the principles of complementary and congeniality of excellences. No one is compelled to join the public system.   In fact, a private learning network can work concomitantly with the public system, and in some cases be integrated into it.

However, freedom does not come without responsibility.   Public educational components must fund their enterprises through monies given to them by the CLNAO, educational foundations, and/or donations.   Also, they must be held accountable for those funds.   Instead of a school board controlling resources, free market mechanisms control the way resources are allocated.   In order to ensure accountability, educational components chartered by the CLNAO are audited and monitored.

Levels of Learning

In addition to the concept of embeddedness is the idea of levels of learning. The three important levels of learning that operate concomitantly are the societal environment, the learning system itself, and the parts that comprise the learning system.

Societal Purposes:
- Create a class of individuals who exhibit the qualities of *noblesse oblige*.
- Provide a learning environment that is global, national, regional, and local in character.

- Create a society in which all spheres of society—political, cultural, economic, and environmental—are arranged and integrated to assist individuals with actualizing their true potentials.

- Strive to maintain the sustainable relationships between the political, cultural, economic, and environmental spheres.

- Protect fundamental human rights.

- Achieve the Greater Good.

Learning System Purposes:

- Organize learning principles, methods, applications, and strategies around the cognitive abilities, interests, and inclinations of each learner.

- Manage the learning system with principles of self-government.

- Integrate nodes of the learning system into other systems.

- Transform the learning system spiritually and operatively.

- Apply free market mechanisms to ensure efficient and effective use of resources.

Constituents Purposes:

- Support learners in their good growth toward their self-actualization.

- Encourage learners to take an active role in their own learning by providing them guidance and support in self-directed learning and self-assessment.

- Provide learners opportunities to interact with their environment and society so they can understand it better and become more adept at adjusting to its changes.

- Provide for learners a wide range of experiences in self-government so they share in the design of their social systems through participatory democratic measures.

Attaining these purposes at each of the levels contains some potential conflicts. One conflict that could arise is determining whose Good is the Greater Good. In communities that are politically charged with intellectual dichotomies, it will require considerable time for generative dialogue to determine whose Good is the Greater Good. In most cases, common ground will be found between individuals and society as a whole.

Another area for potential conflict is in the re-distribution of wealth. Switching from a centralized learning system to a decentralized one is not easy. In a decentralized system, free and fair market mechanisms and the principles of self-actualization assist in distributing goods and utilities. In instituting the new system, some people may fall through the gaps and not receive those goods and utilities to which they are entitled. This can occur if learner reciprocity does not exist, that is, when a system closes itself off from other systems and learners. In order to ensure a just distribution of goods and utilities, systems should be open to one another and employ free market mechanisms in the allocation of goods and utilities.

Boundaries

Figures 19 and 20 on page 218 depict boundaries within the learning system. Boundaries can be of various kinds, such as physical and resource boundaries (ibid., 40-41). The first boundary that can be identified is physical boundaries. In this learning system local and world geography is considered. In order to bring the public network and the world to people, several components are created. At the local level is the ICDO that is in walking distance to people's homes. The ICDO helps community members with advising and curricular development. If a person is interested in learning German and going to Germany for a home-stay, the ICDO helps him arrange a learning experience with an international home-stay organization.

A second boundary is the life stages of childhood, adolescence, maturity, and old age. Unlike the current learning system in which learners only learn with peers of the same age, a transformational system is inter-generational.   For example, a learning pod for children ages six to eight might spend time learning with older children ages nine to twelve.   The rippling effect or tutoring method is one way in which to overcome age boundaries.

Psychological boundaries such as feelings, attitudes, dispositions, and perceptions are a third boundary.   It has been asserted in this paper that not all people learn the same way.   This reality presents a problem-situation for parents and teachers. How does a person teach to all the different learning styles?   To cope with this problem-situation, parents and teachers work with other parents and teachers in the learning system.   This could be parents and teachers of the same learning pod, teachers at the neighborhood ICDO, teachers of CLCs, and researchers in learning styles and approaches.   International, national, regional, and local organizations also enable parents and teachers to network and learn together how to become better teachers in order to overcome the psychological boundaries.

Resource boundaries are a fourth type of boundary with which the system copes. Since resources are limited and learning should take place in alignment with the principles of self-actualization, brain-compatible learning, and self-government, free market mechanisms are utilized in the system. Educational foundations and the CLNAO provide funding to learning system components that do well in the system. A public voucher system is employed in order to measure the quality of development in the system. In order to get resources that may be outside of the system, the CLNAO integrates its voucher system with voucher systems of other learning systems.

Breaks, Inputs, and Outputs

In order for the learning system to routinely interact with other systems, breaks within the system's boundaries are created. These breaks allow the system to receive input from the environment as well as to send output back to it (ibid., 29). This kind of system is called an open system (ibid., 31). One of the principles of systemic design that pertains to the issue of openness is put forth by Banathy as follows: "The more open the system is, the more kinds of input it has to cope with" (ibid., 27). Furthermore, the principle pertaining to output is that in order "to produce output, the system requires input from the environment" (ibid., 29). In order to cope with input, a complex system is created. Under the Principle of Requisite Variety, "a system has to match that variety (complexity) of the environment which is relevant to the system" so it may be a sustainable system (ibid., 32).

Banathy identifies "definition" input, resources, and "noise" as the kinds of input that enter the system. "Definition" input is when "the environment establishes the system—or the system establishes itself in the environment—in order to satisfy certain environmental expectations, demands, and requirements...constraints and rules" (ibid., 29).   The world realities that were identified in Chapter 8 are different kinds of input.   In most cases, communities will already have learning systems in place but will need to transform them into a transformational learning system in order to match them with the realities of today's world.   The Inter-University Futures Collaborative, Futures Institute, and the learning community structure within the individual systems help filter into the local learning system "definition" input.

A second kind of input is resources.   Resources are those goods and utilities that come from the societal environment of the learning system which are necessary for the system to function (ibid., 42).   Such resources include mature persons who come from the community to assist in managing the system or teaching in it.

A third kind of input is what Banathy refers to as *noise*, "a large and unorganized collection of 'undefined' input" (ibid., 29).   One component that deals with noise is The Inter-University Futures Collaborative.   The Collaborative deciphers between "definition" input that helps the system adjust or transform to changes in the environment and input that is undefinable for the system.

Input that the system receives from the environment is transformed into output that is sent back to it.   Banathy has matched the types of input with the types of output. "Definition" output is "the outcome of what the system does...the tangible realization of stated expectations, demands, and requirements that the environment or the system defined as one type of input" (ibid., 29).   The kinds of output from the learning system include learners, new knowledge, products, and services of value to the community and the society (ibid., 42). For example, in the case of the Collaborative, when "definition" input comes into the learning system the Collaborative analyzes it within a futures context and provides scenarios on how the learning system could react. Either the system adjusts to the changes or makes a transformation in order to co-evolve with the environment. This kind of information serves as input for other organizations. Since all human activity systems are conceptualized as learning organizations, these systems will have components to react to change. Any information coming out of the Collaborative would be helpful for these communities in learning about changes that are occurring and how other systems are reacting to these changes.

Resources are those goods and utilities that are "formulated in terms of requests, requirements of resources that the system needs in order to produce the expected output" (ibid., 29). For example, imagine that a new solar system has been discovered by NASA ("DEFINITION" INPUT). Unfortunately, the new solar system can only be seen through a very expensive electromagnetic telescope. Since many people in the community would like to see this new solar system and learn how it relates to this solar system, one of the science CLCs approaches a foundation for funding. This request is the RESOURCE OUTPUT since it is a signal that is sent out into the community for a resource to be used in the learning system.

"Noise" is undefined and "includes unexpected output, waste, noise, etc." (ibid., 29). Banathy contends that in current educational systems waste "includes a large number of students…who have dropped out, been weeded out as undesirable, or cannot perform as expected" (ibid., 42). He calls this "a waste of human potential!" (ibid.).

In this learning system people are not waste. People are both valuable inputs and value-creating outputs. The kinds of things that might be considered waste in the learning system are those things that deter or holdback human potential. These must be found and filtered out of the system in order to maintain the system's vitality and sustainability.

Relationships

In the future learning system there are vertical and horizontal relationships between the different systems and within the learning system itself. Vertical relationships relate to the issue of embeddedness. This is illustrated in Figure 20 on page 218. What is not shown in Figure 20 is the suprasystem of the learning system. The suprasystem is when a particular learning system is embedded within another learning system, for example, a Catholic learning pod or CLC that is embedded within the suprasystem of the Holy Catholic Church. The community is not the suprasystem because the community is not a learning system (ibid., 43). Thus, the learning system is the *system of interest* since it is the primary system (ibid., 44). If it is compared to other local learning systems, then it can be referred to as the *system in focus* because it is viewed in relationship to other systems (ibid.).

Within a suprasystem there are peer systems. Banathy identifies three kinds of peer systems: centralized, egalitarian, and hierarchical (1992). The learning system (suprasystem) designed in this paper is a de-centralized system, but within it there are centralized, egalitarian, and hierarchical sub-systems. An example of a centralized system would be an individual learning pod. It has its own culture and this culture defines its rules, regulations, and ways of learning. An example of an egalitarian system is a group of learning pods. Each pod is different but each pod respects the rights of other pods, and more importantly, interacts with other pods in order to further the self-actualization of all learners. An example of a hierarchical system is the political sphere. Power is derived from the people, as in the case of the CLNAO, and within the CLNAO a chain of command is defined.

Openness and Closedness

The educational system designed in Part 3 is an open system, but it is not a completely open system because, according to Banathy, "a completely open system—one without boundaries—would not be, and could not be, considered to be a system in that it could not have any orderly interaction with the environment" (ibid., 45). Openness and closedness are matters of degree. In this learning system the notion of "closure by control" is applied, which is the ability of the system "to define its boundaries, adjust the breaks on its boundaries, and regulate its input and output" (ibid.).

One example of openness and closedness is the learning system defined within a particular community. This community could be a township, such as Oakville, a school district, such as the Mehlville School District, or a county, such as St. Louis County. If the learning system were to include an entire county, such as St. Louis County, residents would have access to its CLCs and public facilities. If the system were to create a partnership with another county, such as Fenton County, to allow residents of both counties to use each other's CLCs and public facilities, then the two systems would integrate their subsystems into each other, such as the voucher systems. This integration would be a break in St. Louis County's learning system.

The life stages of childhood, adolescence, maturity, and old age also exhibit the characteristics of openness and closedness. Each particular stage of life is attended to by its own learning system, such as childhood education, thus providing boundaries within which to teach and learn. However, each learning system has breaks that allow for inter-generational learning, such as rippling or tutoring. New developments in brain-based learning are another way for breaks to occur within each learning system. For example, Jensen recognizes the stages of preparation, acquisition, elaboration, memory, formation, and functional integration (2000, 31). He identifies other boundaries such as gender differences and functional differences between genders. Gordon Dryden and Colin Rose divide their early childhood learning program into a range of birth to two years that focuses on the senses of hearing, feeling, smelling, tasting, and doing. This range is subdivided into boundaries of birth to six weeks, six weeks to six months, six months to twelve months, and twelve months to eighteen months (Dryden 1995).

Resource boundaries are another kind of boundary that is open but controlled. The voucher system helps control the use of resources. Learners from outside the system cannot use the community resources unless a break exists in the boundary to allow them to have access. One way to provide such a break is to integrate the community voucher system into a voucher system of another community.

Self-Regulation

Not only is the learning system an open system, but it is a self-regulating one. A self-regulating system is sensitive to the changes in the greater environment as well as to changes within the system (ibid., 32). It can either adapt to changes or transform itself into a new system. Banathy defines adaptation as the "capability to respond to environmental changes that are relevant to the life" of the learning system (ibid., 46). It is a process through which errors in the system are identified and modifications are made to bring the system in line with its environment and future expectations (ibid., 47). It adapts to changes when it senses changes in the systemic-environment and receives information from it regarding changed requirements (ibid., 32). It then processes feedback, information that is sent out into the systemic-environment about the deficiencies in the output (ibid.). Negative feedback involves adaptation. It is the deviation between the actual state and the expected state. The system adjusts to this deviation by reducing it (ibid.).

Another way for the system to react to changes is to transform itself into a new system. Transformation is influenced by positive feedback, which is the calling for positive changes in the system or increasing the deviation between the actual state and the expected state. When positive feedback exists, adaptation cannot work since it is unable to provide the necessary match between the system and its environment. The changes in the environment call for a new system to be created that can match it with the new expectations and requirements and create new functions, components, and operations for implementing the system in a manner that allows it to coevolve with the environment and transform when necessary (ibid., 33).

The learning system is a transformational system since the peer systems and their subsystems co-evolve with the environment.   The Inter-University Futures Collaborative and the Futures Institute are two major peer systems.   These components send information into the system regarding changes in the environment and how the other systems may transform, such as replacing CLCs with a new kind of component.

Functions/Structure Model

The Functions/Structure Model is a recapitulation of the issues discussed in Chapters 14 through 17.   It is a snapshot view of the system at a given moment in time (Banathy 1996, 80).   This model can be understood as the mission and purposes of the system on pages 165-167, its specifications on pages 170-173, the functions that carry out the mission and purposes on pages 176-189, the components of the system that attend to the functions on pages 193-196, and finally the relational arrangements of the components as illustrated in Figure 13 on page 200, Figure 14 on page 201, Figure 15 on page 202, Figure 16 on page 204, Figure 17 on page 207, and Figure 18 on page 208.

The Functions/Structure Model creates its functions and structures based upon the mission, purposes, and specifications.   The main functions of the system include 1) providing a learning environment that is global, national, regional, and local in character; 2) supporting learners' growth toward their self-actualization and furnishing them with opportunities to avail themselves to other learners; 3) integrating nodes of the learning system into other systems; 4) transforming the learning system spiritually and operatively; 5) managing the system with principles of self-government; 6) applying free market mechanisms to ensure efficient and effective use of resources; 7) protecting fundamental human rights; 8) balancing the political, cultural, economic, and environmental spheres; and 9) creating the proper learning conditions for people to recognize the Greater Good as well as to explore their own paths in achieving it.

The components that enable the public learning system to implement the functions include those listed within the four spheres of society. Within the political sphere are the CLNAO and its arm the ICDO. Within the cultural sphere are CLCs, learning pods, and other private and civil associations. Within the economic sphere there are firms and businesses. Finally, within the environmental sphere there are human physical systems such as Startech Systems, natural systems such as rivers and lakes, and human systems such as farms and environmental organizations.

Process/Behavioral Model

The Process/Behavioral Model is the model in motion. Unlike the systems-environment model that allows designers to see the system as it is within the context of the community and larger society or the functions/structure model that enables them to view the learning system at a given moment in time, the process/behavioral model projects the system as it operates through time. This is an exciting aspect of the learning system because the model processes can be seen. One way to understand model building is to imagine a black box, such as in Figure 21.

Figure 21.   The Black Box View.

In the previous models the functions, components, inputs, and outputs were identified, but there is no clear conception of their processes.   In this section the black box becomes transparent and its inner workings are seen throughout time.   The learning that takes place in the system occurs through The Learning Cycle and The Learning Matrix.   Using Banathy's General Process/Behavioral Model, a general view of this process is illustrated in Figure 22.   Though Banathy provides more detailed models regarding input processing, transformation processing, output processing, and systems guidance/management, this treatise will only make reference to the general model for simplicity purposes.

Figure 22.   Banathy's General Process/Behavioral Model (1992, 103)

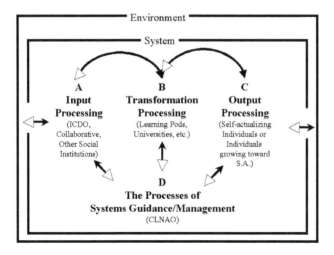

Figure 22 is a general view of the process/behavioral model in terms of the learning system. Banathy identifies four functions of the process/behavioral model, input, transformation, output, and systems guidance/management. Input processing includes those functions and components of the learning system that interact with the environment (ibid., 102). The system identifies and searches for systems-relevant input. The kinds of input that come into the system are definition input, resources, and noise. For this system, definition input means learners and any other relevant information that affects the system. Resources include money, facilities, natural environs, tools, and people. Noise is any input that is not relevant to the system.

Transformation processing includes those functions and components of the learning system that create conditions and activities to transform the input into the desired output and through which the system is maintained, developed, or changed (ibid.). Transformation is specifically concerned with the Learning Cycle and Learning Matrix. As will be explained later, transformation processing occurs even before the learner is identified by the system because learning happens within the household of parents, siblings, relatives, neighbors, and immediate environment. The Learning Cycle is transformational processing within the public learning system.

Output processing includes those functions and components of the learning system that create the conditions and operations which identify and assess the purpose-relevant output and dispatches it into the environment (ibid., 103). As Figure 22 illustrates, the main form of output is self-actualizing individuals or those still in their growth toward self-actualization. Though people may seem to be depicted as some

238

kind of finished product to be sent out into society, like a light bulb, in reality this learning system is not a machine that produces a final product.   Self-actualization is an on-going process and people interact with their society on a daily basis.   It would be misleading to assert that "output" is a final product when in fact it only marks an end of one stage and the beginning of another.

When a learner grows, people interact with him at different points in time of his growth and he is perceived differently at each point in time.   Imagine that it has been two years since I last saw my nephew.   Once I meet him again, I make a quick comparison in my mind of what he was like two years prior with what he is like now. This comparison is a mental construct and is referred to as "output."   My nephew in reality is not a finished product of any kind, but my comparison of him allows me to perceive him as "output."   I see him and say, "Look how Yuki has changed!"

Though not illustrated in Figure 22, another kind of output that the system produces is new knowledge about human growth and development and learning. Parents and teachers on a daily basis assess how children learn.   The data they collect is in turn given to researchers to produce literature on its relevance to the learning system and society in general.   New developments in cognitive science are one example.   Cognitive scientists may look at the data that is produced in learning situations, perform studies in relationship to the data, and then establish their own findings that become new realities.   Experts such as Howard Gardner and his colleagues at Harvard Project Zero make sense of these new realities.   They, in turn, create a vast storehouse of new teaching/learning concepts, methods, and applications based upon their own research that stems from the new developments in cognitive science and human growth and development. This new knowledge then becomes "output" for teachers and society in general. And the cycle continues.

Systems Guidance/Management includes feedback, adjustment, and change. It analyzes and interprets information that is relevant to assessing the processes and outcomes of the learning system, introducing adjustments to the system based upon the analysis and interpretation, and changing or redesigning the system (ibid.). The main component for guiding and managing the public learning system is the CLNAO. It implements a voucher system that facilitates free market mechanisms in the system. It cooperates with the political, cultural, economic, and environmental spheres of society in integrating functions and components in order to provide system clients the best learning experiences possible. It monitors the system to ensure that everyone's basic civil rights are protected and that nobody abuses the system.

In addition to the CLNAO's own monitoring systems, the Inter-University Futures Collaborative and Futures Institute assist the learning system with managing the system by providing their analyses and interpretations of the changes in the societal spheres in relationship to the learning system. This information helps the CLNAO manage these changes and determine if adjustments need to be made or if the system needs to be redesigned.

The arrows in Figure 22 illustrate the recurring four system processes within each of the process domains. Input Processing is a process domain and can be viewed

240

as three interacting arrows.   The arrow that goes from the Input Domain to the

environment represents "input" into the Input Domain.   This "input" is transformed in

the Input Domain (A Black Box).   From the Input Domain the transformed input is

dispatched as an "output" into the Transformation Processing Domain.   The arrow that

goes from Input Processing to Systemic Guidance/Management is the process that

assesses the Input Domain to determine if adjustments need to be made or the Input

Domain needs to be redesigned.

The Learning Cycle and Learning Matrix

The Learning Cycle

Banathy's Process/Behavioral Model can be translated into a simplified

version that is referred to as The Learning Cycle.   The Learning Cycle in Figure 23

illustrates how one learns within a community of learners.

Figure 23. Learning Cycle

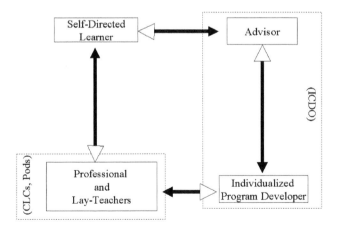

The cycle contains four major components: Self-directed Learner, ICDO, CLCs, and Learning Pods.   The learner is identified by the ICDO as soon as he is considered by the community to be a member.   He is issued by his neighborhood ICDO a voucher identification number and card.   The parents of this child receive from their neighborhood ICDO an information packet explaining the learning system, its learning opportunities, and easy-to-read information booklets on how children learn and how best parents can help them learn.   In addition to these materials, parents receive information in the form of brochures or magazines regarding the relevant learning pods and community learning centers for their child.

Because of the flexibility of the system, people can choose whether or not to attend their neighborhood ICDO after receiving this information.   Some members of the community may be part of sectarian learning systems.   However, even if these people participate in a private learning system, they are still included in the public system in order to offer them more learning opportunities.

Let me address two points that have been raised in discussions regarding the Learning Cycle.   First, the cycle is not rigid even though Figure 23 illustrates it to be so.   It should be thought of as iterative cycles in which the learner moves freely about the learning system.   Because of the advent of technology, advising and learning can take place over the Internet or video conferencing with those teachers, mentors, and guides in the greater community.

Second, parents are not cut out of the picture though they are not illustrated in Figure 23. The child's learning begins in the home and his parents guide him throughout his discovery and exploratory studies and activities. The Learning Cycle is an approach toward expanding the child's learning into the greater community and to assist him in becoming a self-directed learner. Based upon the Principles of Complementarity and Congeniality of Excellences, the community takes responsibility for *assisting* him and his parents with his learning beyond the family. It does not replace the role of parents or takes full control of the child's learning program in order to mold him into something it thinks he should be. If parents decide to participate in the public learning system, they, along with their child, begin consulting with an ICDO curricular advisor. This is different from the classical paradigm of education in which adults dominate and prescribe the learner's experiences. However, it does not mean that the child chooses "willy-nilly" which courses to take in his learning program without parental and teacher advice. Parents and the ICDO curricular advisor guide him in the learning process in order to maintain a level of continuity throughout the learning experience so one activity builds upon another.

When the child and his parents meet with the ICDO curricular advisor, she assists in diagnosing the child. This could be referred to as a "needs analysis." A "needs analysis" helps everyone involved in the learning experience of the child. It is used to discover the child's potential and assist him, his parents, teachers, mentors, and caretakers in guiding and teaching him. Some of the factors involved in the needs analysis include stage of life, prior self-actualizing experiences, multiple intelligences, identification of possible personal inclinations, and other learning experiences.

In order for parents, teachers, mentors, and caretakers to assist the child with setting goals for himself, his stage of life needs to be considered since each stage of life is cognitively different from the next.   The principles of brain-compatible learning, Howard Gardner's theory of multiple intelligences, and Heinz Werner's findings in *Comparative Psychology of Mental Development* address some of the issues that are relevant to this aspect of the analysis.

In addition to the child's stage of life, knowledge about prior self-actualization experiences is important in assisting the learner.   If the learner is already acquainted with a domain, such as music, these experiences are taken into consideration in assisting him with creating an individualized program.   The curriculum developer assesses what he has learned, how well he has learned it, and assists him in determining what learning environments are best for drawing out this potential.

Multiple Intelligences diagnosis is also important for assessment.   Howard Gardner and Joseph Walters in *Multiple Intelligences: The Theory in Practice*, contend that assessment of the intelligences assists learners, parents, adult guides, and caretakers in becoming more aware of a learner's inner potentials.   This awareness helps the child in seeking appropriate environments that are conducive to the drawing out of a particular potentiality.   Though they do suggest diagnostic testing, they do not necessarily subscribe to "paper-and-pen" testing.   They argue that diagnosis should be done holistically.   It should search "for genuine problem-solving or product-fashioning skills in individuals across a range of materials" of the intellectual medium (1993, 31).

A fourth factor involved in assessment is the identification of a learner's possible inclinations.   This is different from knowing prior self-actualizing experiences. In the course of the learning situation or slightly before, the child may show strengths in certain domains of which he or his parents and teachers might be aware.   If this is the case, then his parents and teachers should assist him with developing such an inclination. For example, if a six-year-old boy is identified as gravitating toward music, spending a considerable amount of time with music, and showing ability or extraordinary ability in playing a musical instrument, then this is a sign of a personal inclination toward music.

Finally, other learning experiences help in assessing the learner.   By knowing what things he has or has not had experience with doing, the learner, with the assistance of his parents and teachers, can better develop his learning program.   These experiences might not be inclinations necessarily, but activities that he has done.   The learner may wish to pursue additional activities of the same nature and his parents and teachers should assist him in participating in commensurable learning activities.

After the assessment, the curriculum advisor works with an individualized program developer to screen, select, and evaluate the data from the assessment.   This is both an art and a science.   It requires the ICDO staff to take the following factors into consideration: results of needs analysis (assessment), disciplines of knowledge (what things the child wants to learn), types of learning (how the individual learns best via his multiple intelligences [MI]), learning locations (CLCs, museums, greater environs, etc.), kinds of professional and lay-teachers (Learning pod choice), scope of learning experiences, etc.

After the information has been screened, selected, and evaluated by the curricular advisor and individualized program developer, a consultation takes place. During the consultations, the learner, his parents, and ICDO staff brainstorm various learning situations. The individualized program developer first considers the results of the assessment and the suggestions that the advisor has made concerning program development. Second, the program developer confirms with the learner and his parents the kinds of things he is interested in learning. If they do not know, then the program developer goes through the spectrum of knowledge determining if the child has a particular learning interest.

Another important aspect of this session is how the individual best learns. This would have been determined by the MI assessment. Based on the assessment, the program developer writes a report of suggested learning methods for the child. Using this information, the learner, with the assistance of his advisor and parents, chooses those learning pods and CLCs that are able to meet his distinct learning needs and interests. If the learner enters a pod and later does not like it, he can switch to a different pod.

Finally, the scope of the learning experiences is an important consideration. In order to assist the learner, his parents, and his pod teachers with creating realistic learning objectives for him, the program developer needs to know from the learner and his parents how long he would be interested in doing a particular learning activity. For example, if the child is interested in soccer, the curriculum developer should know if it is to be an afternoon or short-term extra-curricular activity.

During the brainstorming session, the program developer, the learner, and his parents complete a schedule sheet. Computer software is used to develop this educational program. Together they decide which kinds of learning experiences would benefit him toward his good-growth-toward his self-actualization. Next, they browse through a catalog that has categories of learning pods with descriptions. After completing the worksheet, the program developer inputs the information into a matching database. If a learning pod is available, then the child is able to join the pod.

Other possibilities exist for matching learners. If the learner has activity and time constraints, he can still be matched with other learners without having to join a learning pod. He meets with an advisor and program developer at the neighborhood ICDO for an assessment. Together they brainstorm ideas and using a software program they create a learning program worksheet such as Figures 24 and 25. This software screens, selects, and evaluates the input that the learner and program developer have entered into the computer.

Figure 24. Individualized Curriculum Program Worksheet (Input)

Preferred Time	Preferred Day	Learning Activity	Category #	Preferred Location
09:00	M-F	American Culture Studies	005	Kanazawa City CLC
10:00	M-F	Japanese Culture Studies	001	Kanazawa City CLC
11:00	M-F	Computer Graphic Design	132	Kanazawa Institute of Technology
12:00		Lunch		
13:00	M-F	Physical Science: Learning About Motion	234	Naka-machi CLC
14:15	M-F	Environmental Studies: Learning About Living Systems	235	Naka-machi CLC
15:15	M-F	Creative Crafts	345	Naka-machi CLC

Figure 25. Printout of Matching Results (Output)

Time	Day	Learning Activity	Category #	Location	Group #
09:00-10:00	M-F	American Culture Studies	005	Kanazawa City CLC	3
10:10-11:10	M-F	Japanese Culture Studies	001	Kanazawa City CLC	2
11:30-12:30	M-F	Computer Graphic Design	132	Kanazawa Institute of Technology	1
12:30		Lunch			
13:45-14:45	M-F	Physical Science: Learning About Motion	234	Naka-machi CLC	4
15:00-16:00	M-F	Environmental Studies: Learning About Living Systems	235	Naka-machi CLC	4
16:05-17:10	M-F	Creative Crafts	345	Naka-machi CLC	2

In Figure 25 a matching result of the information that was entered into the computer program is created. The group number corresponds to the group for each learning activity. In addition, the computer program places the learner in a group with people who have the same interests from both the neighborhood ICDO and the larger community.   The learner may be with a twelve or twenty-year-old; however, this does not mean that they are doing the same things at the same cognitive levels.   The twenty-year-old may be an intern who wants to work with younger or older people.   Also, because the learner's cognitive abilities may differ from other group members, the group may require more than one professional or lay-teacher to assist learners.   If there is another student of the same age, the teacher may work with both students using a variety of methods to teach and assist with the learning process.

As the printout sheet illustrates, learning does not always occur in neighborhood CLCs.   Activities may take place in several areas throughout the community learning network, such as a neighborhood graphics art institute.   In addition, the student is not locked into any artificial timeframe.   He does not have to finish his learning activities at the same time or complete them at the same location. Timeframes are established based upon the objectives that learner, parents, and educators set together.

The Learning Matrix

The Learning Matrix is an eclectic approach toward the perennial ideas and methods on learning that work to achieve the full development of the individual and the acquisition of knowledge, skills, and virtues for his productiveness in society.   The following figures illustrate the Matrix.

Figure 26.   Core Human Commonalities

Ernest L. Boyer in *The Basic School*, identifies core commonalities or experiences that are common to all people.   He calls these "the essential conditions of human existence" (1995, 85).   These core human commonalities are the life cycle, human symbols, group membership, time and space, aesthetics, nature, production and consumption, and purposeful living (ibid.).   The importance of considering these core human commonalities in education is to enable the learner to gain an understanding and appreciation for each of the cores as well as an understanding of the interrelationships between the cores.   For each core, Boyer has established over-arching goals.

The Life Cycle

Over-arching Goal: Understand the time dimensions of human life: birth, growth, and death.   Acquire a basic understanding of the human body, such as its needs and functions.   Adopt personal habits that lead toward living well and fully.   Develop an appreciation for and understanding of the awe and wonder of life and how life experiences are similar and different between cultures (ibid., 86).

The Use of Symbols

<u>Over-arching Goal</u>: Understand that symbols are a means toward human communication. Explore various aspects of communication, such as history, purposes, technologies, and effects. Discover that integrity is vital to authentic human interaction (ibid., 88).

Membership in Groups

<u>Over-arching Goal</u>: Understand that group membership is part of human community, such as the family. Consider ways in which people affect organizations and organizations affect people. Develop a disposition toward civic and social responsibility (ibid., 90).

A Sense of Space and Time

<u>Over-arching Goal</u>: Understand that people have the mental capacity to imaginatively conceive of themselves in different points on the spectrums of time and space. Explore time through human history and intergenerational connections. Understand national history and learn the cultural traditions of other societies. Learn where other nations and cultures are located in both space and time (ibid., 92).

Response to the Aesthetic

<u>Over-arching Goal</u>: Understand that the artistic expression is an essential quality of the human experience. Learn the different kinds of artistic expression and recognize the benefits of creating art. Learn about the visual and performing arts in different cultures and how they have evolved (ibid., 94).

Connections to Nature

<u>Over-arching Goal</u>: Understand that human beings are an integral part of the natural world.   Become skillful in the use of methods for understanding the natural world, such as the scientific method.   Through interaction with nature learn about its beauties and wonders and nurture in oneself a profound respect for it (ibid., 96).

Producing and Consuming

<u>Over-arching Goal</u>: Understand that within all cultures people produce and consume artifacts.   Develop a disposition toward meaningful work and recognize the value of work in one's life.   Understand the difference between wants and needs.   Understand the importance of information in being an informed consumer and responsible "conserver" (ibid., 98).

Living with Purpose

<u>Over-arching Goal</u>: Understand that within all human societies people seek to understand the meaning of their lives and to actualize their true potentials.   Understand the different values and ethics of one's culture and the importance these play in society. Understand how religion has shaped the human experience.   Begin to understand the significance of charity and service (ibid., 99-100).

Figure 27. Disciplines of Knowledge as They Revolve Around Core Commonalities

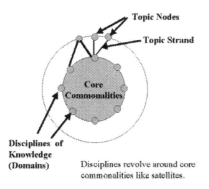

Figure 27 illustrates the revolving elements around the core human commonalities. The disciplines of knowledge[2] revolve around the core human commonalities like satellites. This shows that knowledge is not fixed and that multiple entry points exist for a learner to enter into a core commonality from any of the disciplines or vice-versa. For example, science is a discipline of knowledge or domain. Science can enter into any of the core human commonalities from various angles. In *Wholistic Hands-On Science*, Jerry DeBruin identifies twenty "big ideas of science" and arranges those ideas into twenty learning interdisciplinary packets (LIPS) that contain developmentally appropriate ideas and activities which address the over-arching concepts of science (1995, 9). He lists the ideas along with a discipline topic focus, such as the idea of education being listed with the scientific method. Table 1 depicts one way to conceptualize the relationships between a discipline and a discipline topic in regards to DeBruin's method.

---

[2] Recall Gardner's definition that disciplines or domains are "socially constructed human endeavors...An organized set of activities within a culture, one typically characterized by a specific symbol system and its attendant operations" (1999b, 82).

Table 1. Interrelationships Between Science, Topics, and Other Disciplines

"Big Ideas"	Discipline Topics (Topic Nodes)	Connecting Disciplines
Cycles	Cycles	• Mathematics and Computers • Language Arts • Reading • Music and Creative Drama • Art • Health and Physical Education • Home Economics • Industrial Technology and Crafts • Career Education • Social Studies • Creative Writing • Values
Education	Scientific Method	• Mathematics and Computers • Language Arts • Reading • Music and Creative Drama • Art • Health and Physical Education • Home Economics • Industrial Technology and Crafts • Career Education • Social Studies • Creative Writing • Values

A discipline topic can be referred to as a "topic node." The topic node is connected to the domains by a topic strand. The topic strand connections can be "proto-disciplinary," "interdisciplinary," "multidisciplinary," or "metadisciplinary." Since Gardner contends that it "is simply not feasible for most youngsters during the middle years of childhood, or for most of their teachers" to master two disciplines, he distinguishes between "proto-disciplinary" and "interdisciplinary" (1999a, 219). He defines proto-disciplinary as those things that teachers do with children that they consider to be interdisciplinary but are really a situation in which the teachers "introduce an attractive topic…and allow children to read or write or draw about these topics as they wish" (ibid.).   Interdisciplinary, on the other hand, is the mastering of

two or more disciplines and joining them together in an appropriate manner, a task that

is not possible for most people until college when they have achieved mastery in two or

more disciplines (ibid., 219-220).   Multidisciplinary is when the learner studies a topic

from the points of view of various representatives of the relevant disciplines, such as

when the Renaissance is seen from the views of a historian, literary critic, or musician

(ibid., 220).   Finally, Gardner defines metadisciplinary as the "actual discussion of the

nature of disciplines and how they might be combined," such as when a physicist and a

mathematician get together to discuss the natures of physics and mathematics and how

they are integrated (ibid.).

        With an understanding of core human commonalities, disciplines of knowledge,

topic nodes, and topic strands, teachers and parents can assist the child with creating an

individualized curriculum.   How his program is designed depends upon his age and

cognitive abilities.   For example, a child of two to five years will be concerned more

with selecting activities and performing them than with the logistics of program

development because he is not capable of understanding issues such as curriculum,

design, or subjects.   As Dewey emphasizes in *The Child and the Curriculum*,

"classification is not a matter of child experience; things do not come to the individual

pigeonholed" (1990, 184).   He tells teachers to "abandon the notion of subject-matter

as something fixed and ready-made in itself, outside the child's experience; cease

thinking of the child's experience as also something hard and fast; see it as something

fluent, embryonic, vital" (ibid., 189).

With this in mind, a child between these ages requires learning environments that allow teachers and parents to meet the over-arching goals of the core human commonalities as well as those learning goals for this particular stage of life. However, it does not mean abandoning the notions of the disciplines. It simply means arranging things around the learner: "To the growth of the child all studies are subservient; they are instruments valued as they serve the needs of growth" (ibid., 187). When teachers and parents think of curriculum they should think of two sides, the teacher's side and the pupil's side (Tanner 1997, 47). Teachers and parents are responsible for translating pedagogical issues into meaningful learning experiences for the child and helping him to select and arrange those activities into a set of commensurable activities. The learner is responsible for selecting and arranging learning activities and performing them according to the agreed upon learning goals and objectives in his program. Figure 28 helps in conceptualizing the issues which teachers and parents should consider when arranging learning activities and environments around a learner's particular interests and needs.

Figure 28.   Curriculum Issues

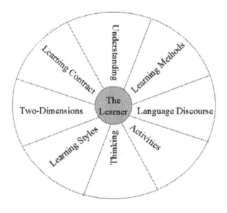

The first issue is where the learner is in his learning, i.e. his stage of life and his cognitive abilities.   This understanding is referred to as the vertical side of the curriculum as illustrated in Figure 29.   The disciplines of knowledge are the horizontal curriculum.   The colored bar on the graph represents a topic node.

Figure 29.   Two-Dimensional Curriculum

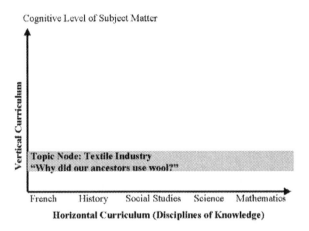

In addressing the two-dimensional curriculum, the case of a six-year-old boy can be considered.   Imagine he joins a learning pod within walking distance to his home. From the teachers' viewpoint they wish to address each of the core human commonalities as well as other pedagogical issues pertaining to each child's growth. Since the community has a wool factory and is connected directly to the children's lives, the teachers decide to use wool as the discipline topic or theme.

The topic node wool cuts across several disciplines.   The teachers in the learning pod work with various CLCs in the neighborhood to help them address this topic node so that the children can learn about wool holistically. This means that learning pod and CLC teachers cooperate to introduce subject matter in a congruent manner so that the children can learn particular concepts and gain particular skills. This goes to the heart of the principles of self-actualization and symbolic interactionist social psychology. Dewey's principle of self-realization, as presented in *Ethics*, asserts that happiness depends upon an individual's "good acts," and each act builds upon future acts. Thus, from an early age an individual needs experiences in performing "good" acts in order to develop the wisdom that will guide him in choosing future "good" acts in later life.

The curriculum is also in alignment with Dewey's Theory of Experience that he puts forth in *Experience and Education*: "The belief that all genuine education comes about through experience does not mean that all experiences are genuinely or equally educative" (1997b, 25). Furthermore, to judge if the experience is educative one must look at the *quality* of the experience. This is measured by those commensurable acts that the individual performs. The quality of an experience has two important aspects: ability to be agreeable to the learner and ability to be commensurable with future acts (ibid., 27-28).

> There is an immediate aspect of agreeableness or disagreeableness, and there is its influence upon later experiences. The first is obvious and easy to judge. The *effect* of an experience is not borne on its face. It sets a problem to the educator. It is his business to arrange for the kind of experiences which, while they do not repel the student, but rather engage his activities are, nevertheless, more than immediately enjoyable since they promote

having desirable future experiences…Wholly independent of desire and intent, every experience lives on in further experiences. Hence the central problem of an education based upon experience is to select the kind of present experiences that live fruitfully and creatively in subsequent experiences.

It has been declared up to this point that learning revolves around the learner and that his learning is his path toward self-actualization. In order to implement this personal transformation, a two-dimensional curriculum is established. It is developed with the understanding that the learner engages the core human commonalities and disciplines through educative acts that are in alignment with his inclinations and that spur on future acts in order to provide continuity toward his learning. For those assisting the child in developing his curriculum, this task is both a science and an art.

Exactly how the curriculum is created depends upon how the learning contract is arranged, that is, how understanding, thinking, language discourse, learning styles, and activities are addressed. According to Malcolm Knowles, a learning contract is "a binding agreement between two or more persons or parties" (1975, 26). It lists the purpose for which the contract is being made, the learning objectives, learning resources and strategies, evidence of accomplishment, and criteria and means of validating evidence (ibid., 62-63). Though Knowles follows an approach that is designed for adult self-directed learners, a learning contract can be created for individuals at any stage in their lives. It is suggested that the contract contain at least the following elements:

1. Name of learner

2. Purpose of Contract, such as "Year Long Program"

3. Program Description

4. Calendar

5. The Curriculum

   a. Overarching Understanding Goals

   b. Learning Objectives

   c. Understanding Performances

   d. Ongoing Assessments

   e. List of Some of the Learning Activities

   f. Learner's Expectations

   g. Teachers' Expectations

   h. Parents' Expectations

The learning contract leads into issues of curriculum design, understanding, and thinking. One approach toward these issues that is becoming popular among teachers in the United States, and that is appropriate for a transformational learning system, is Harvard University's Project Zero's Teaching for Understanding (TfU) Framework and The Thinking Classroom (TC) Framework. The TfU framework is a learning framework within which a two-dimensional curriculum can be established and TC is a means toward understanding. Thus, thinking and understanding are inseparable activities for the learner but are separated here in order to explain their dimensions.

According to the TfU Project at Harvard's Project Zero, understanding is "a matter of being able to do a variety of thought-provoking things with a topic, such as explaining, finding evidence and examples, generalizing, applying, analogizing, and representing the topic in new ways" (Blythe 1998, 12).   This view of understanding is a "performance perspective."   The key aspects of a TfU framework include generative topics, understanding goals, performances of understanding, and ongoing assessment. One of the benefits of this approach is that it can be used within any discipline for any age level[3].   Another benefit is that children and their parents can learn to use the TfU framework and collaborate with teachers on developing the generative topics, understanding goals, performances of understanding, and assessment criteria.

The issue of thinking is inseparable from understanding.   Not only do parents and teachers help the child to understand but they also help him to think.   This is what Harvard Project Zero refers to as a "Thinking Classroom" (TC).   TC is an "environment in which several factors—language, values, expectations, and habits— work together to express and reinforce the enterprise of good thinking" (Tishman et al. 1995, 2).   In creating a TC environment, six dimensions of thinking are addressed: 1) a language of thinking, 2) thinking dispositions, 3) mental management, 4) the strategic spirit, 5) higher order knowledge, and 6) transfer.   Furthermore, in addressing these six dimensions four approaches are always followed: modeling, explaining, interacting, and feedback.

---

[3] I developed with students of Kanazawa Institute of Technology Kobayashi Lab an Internet Portfolio System referred to as SCLL MIILS (Student-centered Language Learning Multimedia Interactive Information Learning System) that served as my TIU internship.   This system allowed teachers to develop learning materials, activities, and projects and record and assess students' learning.   This later incorporated the TfU Framework in the academic years of 2000-2001.   Harvard University's Education with New Technologies has a site for teachers to develop on-line curricula using the TfU framework (http://learnweb.harvard.edu/ent/home/).

The TC Project defines a language of thinking as "the terms and concepts used in the classroom to talk about thinking, and how the language used by the teachers and students in the classroom can work to encourage more high-level thinking" (ibid., 2-3). Thinking dispositions are "students' attitudes, values, and habits of mind concerning thinking, and what the classroom environment can do to promote provocative patterns of intellectual conduct" (ibid., 3).   Five kinds of thinking dispositions are required for good thinking: be curious and questioning, think broadly and adventurously, reason clearly and carefully, organize one's thinking, and give thinking time (ibid., 41-42). Another kind of disposition that could be added is the **disposition to think systemically**, characterized by the ability to see multiple connections and consider the aspects of those connections and their synergistic relationships.

Mental management is a third dimension of thinking.   Learners learn how to be aware of their own thinking processes and teachers consider how to create a classroom culture that encourages students to control their thinking more creatively and effectively (ibid., 3).   The fourth kind of thinking dimension is strategic spirit.   It is an attitude that is fostered within a culture of thinking and that encourages learners to build and use thinking strategies when engaging problem-situations (ibid.).   The fifth thinking dimension is higher order knowledge.   It focuses on knowledge and its applications for solving problems, using evidence, and making inquiries in a discipline (ibid.).   Finally, the dimension of transfer is the application of knowledge and strategies from one learning context to another and the exploration of how different disciplines of knowledge are connected with each other (ibid.).

Two other issues that are important for curriculum development include learning styles and learning methods.   Learning styles pertain to the multiple intelligences that Howard Gardner recognizes.   He defines the eight intelligences in *Intelligence Reframed* (1999b), as follows:

1. *Linguistic*: "Sensitivity to spoken and written language, the ability to learn languages, and the capacity to use language to accomplish certain goals" (ibid., 41).

2. *Logical-mathematical*: "The capacity to analyze problems logically, carry out mathematical operations, and investigate issues scientifically" (ibid., 42).

3. *Musical*: "Skill in the performance, composition, and appreciation of musical patterns" (ibid.).

4. *Bodily-kinesthetic*: "The potential of using one's whole body or parts of the body...to solve problems or fashion products" (ibid.).

5. *Spatial*: "The potential to recognize and manipulate the patterns of wide space...as well as the patterns of more confined areas" (ibid.).

6. *Interpersonal*: "A person's capacity to understand the intentions, motivations, and desires of other people and, consequently, to work effectively with others" (ibid., 43).

7. *Intrapersonal*: "The capacity to understand oneself, to have an effective working model of oneself—including one's own desires, fears, capacities—and to use such information effectively in regulating one's own life" (ibid.).

8. *Naturalist*: The capacity to recognize and classify "the numerous species—the flora and fauna—of his or her environment" and possessing "the talent of caring for, taming, or interacting subtly with various living creatures" (ibid. 48-49).

Furthermore, Gardner suggests several ways in which one can learn via MI. In *Multiple Intelligences: Theory in Practice* (1993), he discusses five ways in which subject matter could be taught.

1. *Narrational Entry Point*: Presenting a story or narrative about the concept under study (ibid., 203).

2. *Logical-Quantitative Entry Point*: Approaching the concept through the use of numerical considerations or deductive reasoning processes (ibid.).

3. *Foundational Entry Point*: Examining the philosophical and terminological aspects of the concept (ibid.).

4. *Esthetic Approach*: Learning through sensory or surface features that appeal to learners who gravitate toward an artistic stance to life (ibid., 204).

5. *Experimental Approaches*: Learning via a "hands-on" approach that uses materials which embody or convey the concept (ibid.).

In addition to these entry points, the authors of *Project Spectrum: Early Learning Activities* (1998), identify eight entry points to understanding: a) mechanics and construction activities, b) science activities, c) music activities, d) movement activities, e) math activities, f) social understanding activities, g) language activities, and h) visual arts activities.

These learning styles and approaches can be matched with learning methods that Moffett recognizes in *The Universal Schoolhouse*. These include universal learning activities that encompass both spontaneous ways of learning and deliberate learning methods (1994, 160-161). Spontaneous learning is witnessing, attuning, imitating, helping, collaborating, and interacting (ibid.). Deliberate learning methods are experimenting, transmitting, transferring "language through knowledge or other symbols," investigating, and apprenticing (ibid.).

Other learning methods include rippling, "an informal, continuous tutorial of some knowledge or skill that everybody is at once receiving from the more experienced and transmitting it in turn to the less experienced" (ibid., 168); tutoring and coaching; apprenticing and interning; visiting, actually visiting new places or people; community service; playing games; therapy; practicing the arts, such as dancing or photography; and spiritual disciplines, such as devotion and discipleship; and home-schooling (ibid., 170-194).

Finally, two other curriculum issues are important to the Learning Matrix: language discourse and activities. Language, whether it is a "language of thinking" or a "language of communication," should be brought to the level of the learner. Parents and teachers should communicate ideas, knowledge, and skills in a language that the learner understands. This language is then made applicable for real learning activities. Recall that learning activities are commensurable activities. The learner should proceed from one activity to the next in order to develop in several dimensions.

It requires several teachers, the support of parents, and resources to assist the learner in creating and implementing a curriculum that develops him at all dimensions. The curriculum should be created with the assistance of a group of teachers from various specialties coming together to develop the learner at his current stage of life. In addition, parents should assist their child with making the plan of study and doing activities with him at home or in the greater community. The learning activities that are used revolve around his development. Because of the Principle of Complementarity of Excellences, members in the learning community contribute to the development of these activities. These can be created with advanced technologies such as SCLL MIILS. By employing such technologies, activities and materials can be developed and used by a variety of teachers, parents, and learners in a variety of ways, catalogued for easy access, and ranked according to usage, preference, or satisfaction.

This discussion connects with Banathy's systemization/integration part of transformational production (1992, 115). In this alternative learning system the more learning at the individual level is carried out in light of self-actualization and the more functions and resources are integrated, the more this synergy represents the greater system. Hence, the call for learning standards does not come from the top but from the bottom. People will come to know what constitutes "good education" because standards of learning will have been created by the daily interactions between people in the learning community.

Standards—Output and Systems Guidance

Each person in the learning system is a self-directed learner within the context of his stage of life and cognitive abilities. In order to evaluate the success of his self-directed learning, various learning assessment tools are applied, such as *processfolios*, "portfolios that encourage students to focus and reflect on their own learning process" (NEA 1993, 3). Learning standards are developed from the bottom-up, not the top-down. For a learner, his parents, and his teachers to determine if he has attained and developed the knowledge, understanding, skills, dispositions, values, and attitudes necessary for his personal growth, standards should be developed around him. These standards are based upon generally acceptable standards of learning that are developed within the learning community. Thus, in order for this learning system to fulfill the second principle, "Organize learning principles, methods, applications, and strategies around the cognitive abilities, interests, and inclinations of each learner," learners, parents, and teachers require the necessary freedoms to identify and assess learning effectively.

It is not the purpose of this dissertation to explain how the learning system determines what is "a good" education or what Banathy refers to as the "desired output" of the learning system. A good education should be defined in terms of what a person decides is the good life for him. In other words, "Does the learning system provide the conditions, goods, and utilities for each member to achieve what he considers to be the good life?" In order to ascertain an answer to this question, those in the learning system who are responsible for guiding the learning process of individuals should interview or survey them according to "satisfaction standards." For example, they could be asked, "Are you satisfied with the help from your ICDO advisor?" or "Are you satisfied with your progress in achieving your learning goals and objectives?"

If the system is not providing the conditions, goods, and utilities for its members to achieve the good life, then either it is going to have to make adjustments or transform those components and/or systems so it does. In communities all across the United States today, several social institutions, such as the local school district, are in place that have the potential to become integral parts of a transformational learning system. However, these systems will need to be transformed, not adjusted. This calls for a radical shift in one's thinking. The approaches suggested in this treatise are one way that communities can transform their social institutions into learning communities.

Part 5

Conclusion

*On the Road Toward Community Sustainability
and Self-Reliance*

Conclusion: On the Road Toward Community Sustainability and Self-Reliance

The purpose of using a systemic design approach was twofold—first, to create a community learning network and second, to demonstrate the applicability of systemic design architecture in the creation of meaningful life-long, life-centered, and self-directed learning communities that are based upon an ethics of self-actualization and democratic, self-government.

Banathy recognizes an unfortunate truth about the professional educational community and the area of systemic design (1996, xi).

> The professional educational community is probably the last—among all other professions—to "get interested in the systems idea." It has failed to embrace systems thinking and has resisted viewing the educational enterprise as a social system. While there has been a proliferation of graduate programs in instructional systems technology, which is conceptualized on closed systems and systems engineering notions, one can seldom find courses on systems thinking—much less on systems theory or methodology—in the catalogues of schools of education.

Despite this unawareness of systemic design in mainstream schools of education, this treatise has held true to the holistic and democratic view of education that The International University (TIU) Asia-Pacific Centers espouse. This perspective is described by graduate colleague Motoshi Suzuki in his article, "The International University, Japan," as an "ecologically oriented concept of community-based learning" with the task of assisting members of a society in creating "a future based on democratic ideals and values" (2000, 80).

This brings the discussion toward an understanding of the university that was described earlier in this paper, especially Alfred North Whitehead's assertion that "Fools act on imagination without knowledge; pedants act on knowledge without imagination" (1967, 93).   It is in reference to Whitehead's chapter, "Universities and Their Function" in *The Aims of Education*, that I ground my conclusions.   Though Whitehead discusses the university and its purposes within his own realm of experiences at the founding of the Harvard University School of Business, he purports that the university should "weld together imagination and experience" (ibid.).

> The justification for a university is that it preserves the connection between knowledge and the zest of life, by uniting the young and the old in the imaginative consideration of learning. The university imparts information, but it imparts it imaginatively.   At least, this is the function which it should perform for society.   A university which fails in this respect has no reason for existence.   This atmosphere of excitement, arising from imaginative consideration, transforms knowledge.

As Banathy has asserted, modern schools of education have not yet acknowledged the importance of systemic design in education, and thus have left out an important tool in developing imagination.   Recall that the mission and purposes of the learning system developed in Part 4 were preceded by the activity of creating an image of the learning system based upon visions, values, and core ideas, i.e. IMAGINATION.   Today's institutions of higher education have not struck a proper balance between imagination and knowledge when discussing learning systems; and this contributes to the dilemma in which many American public educational systems find themselves today.

However, The International University does recognize the importance of imagination and helps to develop it and the knowledge upon which a scholar's work depends.   As Suzuki records from his experiences with his educational program, TIU emphasizes the following (2000, 85):

- Personal study, research, writing and projects...

- Meetings with one or more other persons to discuss ideas, insights, and issues being studied, to make presentations and give feedback.

- Participation in study groups and seminars arranged by the learner and faculty monitor.

- Learning encounters within the learner's community...

- Regional workshops, short courses, and conferences in which learners, mentors, monitors, and other resource persons and specialists in a given geographic area gather to share the outcomes of their individual studies and life journeys, and during which learners have the opportunity to make presentations, receive feedback, and try out new ideas.

To build upon Suzuki's observations, TIU has some of the characteristics of the learning system that I am advocating.   My own experiences with the doctoral program at TIU epitomize the kind of learning that should take place in a public community learning network.   TIU is a network of learning centers throughout the globe, each specializing in its own area of study.   In the case of TIU Asia-Pacific Centers, operation costs are low because there are no large facilities or overhead.   Through special arrangements with other institutions, TIU Asia-Pacific has access to offices, seminar rooms, and/or libraries.   Furthermore, my learning has been an individualized, self-directed learning program that builds upon my experiences while teaching English at the junior high school and university.   My doctoral program is similar to Whitehead's description of the technical apprenticeship in which the preparation of my intellectual career is done "by promoting the imaginative consideration of the various general principles underlying [my] career…connecting details with general principles" (1967, 96).

An alternative framework for community learning centers in the twenty-first century should employ an individualized learning philosophy similar to that of TIU's learning network in which knowledge and imagination are found to be commensurate aspects of the learning endeavor and vital to its sustainability.   Communities should not be misled to believe that their learning organizations, such as CLCs or Learning Pods, should be run like businesses in order to make them accountable to the public; this will only sacrifice imagination in the name of outcome-based learning.   Accountability in a learning organization is measured by a different standard—good teaching, publishing, and/or both.

Good teaching is measured by the originality of the teacher's ideas and her methods of intercourse with learners in helping them to understand key concepts and achieve their agreed upon performances of understanding.   The voucher system described in Chapter 17 helps in measuring this because CLCs or Learning Pods that are performing well will have learners.   The only measure of accountability necessary for teacher performance is the satisfaction of the learner and/or his parents about the learning experience gained.

Publishing should be measured by the teacher meeting her quota of contributions in thought to her discipline (ibid., 99). Whitehead argues that in order to have imaginative teachers, they require times for research (ibid., 97). My own teaching experiences support this assertion. As a teacher, I have grown more as a result of doing research and applying those ideas in the classroom. Professional teachers in the learning system proposed here should been seen no differently than professors at university in respect to the balance between research and application. In alignment with Reigeluth, I argue that teachers should have sabbaticals so that they can make a contribution to their fields and grow as persons. How these sabbaticals are organized will be for each learning organization to decide. But the standard that should be applied regarding professional publications is a quota that Whitehead refers to as one that is "estimated in weight of thought, not in number of words" (ibid., 99).

Though this dissertation describes a particular learning system for public education, it is only one of many possible design solutions for a transformational learning society. There is no one road toward community sustainability and self-reliance. There are certain principles to which any community should adhere in designing its learning system, such as self-actualization and self-government, or certain techniques to employ, such as Rick Smyre's "Capacities for Transformation." However, it is the *imaginative* task of the community to determine what kind of public learning system to create.

In closing, the road toward community sustainability and self-reliance is not found solely by the knowledge of the "road map" that exists today, but also the imagination of the road map that should exist tomorrow. This knowledge is the realities that people confront in everyday life; and using tools such as Banathy's systemic design, Smyre's "Capacities for Transformation," or Fried's "Empowerment," they can create their future road maps. In addition, the creation of the future should occur within a framework of self-actualization and democratic, self-government. Every member of the *polis* has not only a right, but also an obligation to participate and contribute to the ongoing development and sustenance of his community in accordance with his own nature and abilities.

Appendix

Inter-University Futures Collaborative

A Working Paper

by Michael Reber

Copyright © 1999

Introduction

Advancing the concept of the Community Learning Center (CLC) to the level of tertiary education yields a very unique structure. This structure employs those capacities for transformation that Rick Smyre[1] refers to in his paper, *Beyond The Deck Chairs*—process leadership, electronic infrastructure, futures context, 21ˢᵗ century skills for neighborhood leaders, and 21ˢᵗ century concept of the common good. As a result, the educational structure has a different focus from that of the modern university. Instead of placing emphasis on the needs of the institution, it focuses on the development of innovative ideas, methods, and applications for community life in the 21ˢᵗ century and beyond. In addition, there is more cooperation and networking among universities. Finally, curricular development changes. Department designed curricula is transformed into individualized curricula. This shift from the institution to the individual frees up resources, allows for innovation, and provides faculty and students more opportunities to explore and advance their fields.

---

[1] Smyre, Rick. *Beyond The Deck Chairs*, http://www.bev.net/cotf/articles/deck_chairs.html

Description

The new university educational structure that I am describing is what I call the *Inter-University Futures Collaborative.* This collaborative is a group of university learning centers that exists in a sustainable community which operates within an individualized curricular context with emphasis on the development of innovative ideas, methods, and applications for community life in the 21ˢᵗ century and beyond. Though students are enrolled in individualized curricular programs, no one university in the Collaborative serves as a primary institution of study. Instead, students choose faculty advisors from one or more of the learning centers in the Collaborative to develop their curricula. Students have access to multiple learning centers, their resources, collaborative affiliates, and main campuses of the Collaborative universities. Classes and lab or project teams are formed based upon the students' similar learning needs.

Funding of the Collaborative is another unique feature. Since the Collaborative is part of a sustainable community, community taxes go toward its support. For those who are permanent residents[2] of the community, partial tuition wavers are given. The purpose for this is to encourage community members to participate in the Collaborative's educational opportunities that help them to advance their learning and to *think* about the future needs of the community. Those who are not permanent community members pay full tuition to the Collaborative. The tuition revenue is divided among the universities based upon their investments into the Collaborative. An Investment-Revenue Specifications Table is referred to for determining the percentage of return for all universities within the Collaborative. Any

---

[2] Each community would have to decide what constitutes a permanent resident.

returns that are not received by the universities are reinvested into the Collaborative for

operating expenses, projects, and grants to collaborative universities.

Example of An Investment-Revenue Specifications Table

Investment	Return Based Upon 6 Universities
Human Capital (Faculty/Student Ratio. A Higher Ratio Should Allow for a Higher Return)	Faculty/Student Ratio 1:1 = 25% Return 2:1 = 40% Return 3:1 or greater =50% Return
Library of More than 500 Books; Number and Quality of Periodical, Journal, and Newspaper Subscriptions; Quality of Reference Assistance	25% Return
Facilities (Computer Labs, Science Labs, etc.)	15% Return
Other Services (Main Campus Community Life Programs, Access to Main Campus Facilities, etc.)	10% Return

In addition, the following formulas could be used:

Net Income Formula

Gross Revenue per University = Gross Tuition Revenue $\div$ # Of Universities in

Collaborative

Net Income for University = Gross Revenue per University * % Return on Investment

Collaborative Income Formula

Collaborative Income = Total Gross Revenue per University – Total Net Revenue per

University

Collaborative Projects & Grant Income Formula

Collaborative Projects & Grant Income = Collaborative Income – Collaborative

Operating Expenses

Benefits

I have identified at least four benefits of the inter-university futures collaborative.

1. *Ability to Do More with Less*: Each university pools its resources and shares them throughout the Collaborative.

2. *Comparative Advantage*: Each university can concentrate on those things it can do best in terms of community and student needs.

3. *Complementarity of Excellences*: More unique opportunities are created as a more diverse faculty and student population interacts and complements one another's excellences.

4. *Creation of an Experimental Community*: The Collaborative is more than a learning community, it is an experimental community with a focus on the future. Projects and publications that come out of the Collaborative assist communities throughout the world.

Diagram: Six Universities Form a Collaborative

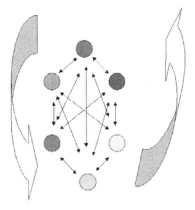

The diagram illustrates the integrated and dependent relationships between each of the six learning centers.   The six arrows represent many things.   They show the paths that students may take throughout the learning centers.   They also illustrate resource flows between the centers—flow of people, ideas, projects, money, and innovations.   The larger flow-arrows around the Collaborative represent the community within which the Collaborative exists.   People, ideas, and resources flow in-and-out of the Collaborative.   Based upon this diagram, the Collaborative can be perceived as a sustainable structure supporting a sustainable community.

Differences between the CLC and Collaborative

Though both the CLC and the Collaborative are integral mechanisms in a sustainable community, they do have differences.   The most visible differences between the CLC and the Collaborative are the levels and kinds of learning that occur as well as the types of sociality that take place.

Learning at the Collaborative is both highly independent and social.   No longer are people dependent upon their parents for assistance regarding educational choices. At this level, individuals are mature enough to make their own decisions, but with guidance from faculty advisors.   Students go about learning what things are available for them to learn and to try to match those resources with their interests.   However, this learning does not take place in a vacuum.   Students will be matched with other students who have similar interests and/or learning needs.   Groups will be formed, subjects studied and discussed, and projects created and carried out.

A note about the socialization process of the Collaborative: Children and adolescents experience a different kind of socialization[3] than do mature individuals. Children and adolescents experience *antecedent sociality*—a **received** sociality to which the person **is responsible**.   On the other hand, mature individuals experience *consequent sociality*—a sociality for which an individual **shares responsibility**. Children and youth are at a stage where they do not yet know who they are.   They are still experiencing life and learning about it.   However, mature individuals have discovered who they are and have decided a course that they will take in their lives. They are now responsible for creating and sustaining community, and they share this responsibility with other mature individuals.   Consequent sociality is prevalent in a Collaborative, and it is a conscious aspect of the learning environment.   Faculty members and students are highly aware of their duty to the community and to themselves.   They know that they are the ones who are the caretakers of the present and the architects of the future.

---

[3] Refer to David Norton's *Personal Destinies*, Princeton University Press, 1976, p. 253, 305.

Conclusion

The insights into the concept of the Community Learning Center help us to envision education beyond the adolescent years.   No longer do we need to think that the purpose of a secondary education is to prepare youth for the world or for college. Instead, education in the adolescent years should be thought of as a means to assist youth with learning about the culture of the community, its symbols, and its needs.   In addition, education should assist youth with identifying and developing those innate qualities or abilities that can help the community and youth to actualize their potentials. Thus, university education is thought of as an ongoing process that was begun with the CLC.

Because of the transformational learning that is begun at the CLC, universities will need to become more cooperative with one another and the communities they serve. They will need to form collaborative efforts like the *Inter-University Futures Collaborative* that I am proposing.

Bibliography

Bibliography

ABC News Website. "Community Centers Seen As Not Fulfilling Their Mission."
11 February 2000. 14 February 2000.
<http://abcnews.go.com/wire/Politics/ap20000211_523.html>.

Adair, Douglas G. 1964. *The Intellectual Origins of Jeffersonian Democracy: Republicanism, the Class Struggle, and the Virtuous Farmer.* Edited by Mark E. Yellin with a Forward by Joyce Appleby. Lanham, Maryland: Lexington Books, 2000.

Andrade, Heidi Goodrich. "Using Rubrics to Promote Thinking and Learning." *Educational Leadership* 57, 5 (February 2000): 13-18.

Appleby, Joyce. *Capitalism and a New Social Order: The Republican Vision of the 1790s.* New York, New York: New York University Press, 1984.

---. *Liberalism and Republicanism in the Historical Imagination.* Cambridge: Harvard University Press, 1992.

Archer, L.B. Quoted in *Designing Social Systems in a Changing World* by Bela Banathy. New York, New York: Plenum Press, 1996.

Aristotle. "Nicomachean Ethics." *The Pocket Aristotle.* Translated by W.D. Ross and edited by Justin D. Kaplan. New York, New York: Washington Square Press, 1958.

---. "Politics." *The Pocket Aristotle.* Translated by Benjamin Jowett and edited by Justin D. Kaplan. New York, New York: Washington Square Press, 1958.

Arons, Stephen. *Short Route to Chaos: Conscience, Community, and the Re-Constitution of American Schooling.* Amherst: University of Massachusetts Press, 1997.

Banathy, Bela H. *Systems Design of Education: A Journey to Create the Future.* Englewood Cliffs, N.J.: Educational Technology Publications, 1991.

---. *Systems View of Education: Concepts and Principles for Effective Practice.* Englewood Cliffs, N.J.: Educational Technology Publications, 1992.

---. *Designing Social Systems in a Changing World.* New York, New York: Plenum Press, 1996.

Becker, Howard S. and Michael M. McCall, editors. *Symbolic Interaction and Cultural Studies.* Chicago: University of Chicago Press, 1990.

Bethel, Dayle, M. *Makiguchi, The Value Creator: Revolutionary Japanese Educator and Founder of Soka Gakkai.* New York, New York: Weatherhill, Inc., 1973, paperback edition, 1994.

---. "The Role of Work in Personality Development and Holistic Learning."
Encounter: Education for Meaning and Social Justice 11 (September 1998): 52-
58.

Bethel, Dayle M., ed., and translated by Alfred Birnbaum.   *Education for Creative
Living: Ideas and Proposals of Tsunesaburo Makiguchi (Soka Kyokikugaku Taikei,
1930)*, by Tsunesaburo Makiguchi.   Ames, Iowa: Iowa State University Press,
1989.

Blumer, Herbert.   *Symbolic Interactionism: Perspective and Method.*   Englewood
Cliffs, New Jersey: Prentice-Hall, Inc., 1969.

Blythe, Tina and et al.   *The Teaching for Understanding Guide.*   San Francisco:
Jossey-Bass Publishers, 1998.

Boulding, K.   Quoted in *Designing Socials Systems in a Changing World* by Bela
Banathy.   New York, New York: Plenum Press, 1996.

Boyer, Ernest L.   *The Basic School: A Community for Learning.*   San Francisco,
California: Jossey-Bass Publishers, 1995.

Brigham v. State.96-502 (Filed 05 February 1997).

Caine, Renate Nummela and Geoffrey Caine. *Making Connections: Teaching and the Human Brain.* New York, New York: Addison-Wesley Publishing Company, 1994.

Campbell, Clyde. "Frank Manley: Leader, Creator, Humanist." *The Evolution of the Community School Concept: The Leadership of Frank J. Manley.* Fairfax, Virginia: National Community Education Association, 1999.

Center for Urban Education, New York, New York. "Ways of Establishing and Funding Community Learning Centers." November 30, 1971a. ERIC Document: ED 091 480.

---. "Educational Leadership Development Program Progress Report." November 30, 1971b. ERIC Document: ED 091 480.

---. "Parent Participation Component of Citizen Participation Program Progress Report." November 15, 1971c. ERIC Document: ED 091 480.

---. "School-Community Relations Component of Citizen Participation Program." November 5, 1971d. ERIC Document: ED 091 480.

---. "Evaluation of the Concept and History of the Community Learning Center." September 1971e. ERIC Document: ED 091 480.

---. "Evaluation of the Educational Leadership Development Component, 1970-71." 1971f. ERIC Document: ED 091 480.

---. "Evaluation of the 1970-71 Parent Participation Workshop Program." 1971g. ERIC Document: ED 091 480.

---. "Evaluation of the Community School Relations Workshop Program 1970-71." 1971h. ERIC Document: ED 091 480.

Centre Songhaï Website. Centre Songhaï Organization. 01 August 1998. 26 February 2001 <http://members.nbci.com/_XMCM/SONGHAI/acceuil.html>.

---. Centre Songhaï Organization. 01 August 1998. 26 February 2001 <http://members.nbci.com/_XMCM/SONGHAI/publication-english.html >.

Charon, Joel M. *Symbolic Interactionism: An Introduction, An Interpretation, An Integration, Sixth Edition*. Upper Saddle River, New Jersey: Prentice-Hall Inc., 1998.

Clark, David. *Schools as Learning Communities: Transforming Education*. London: Cassell, 1996.

Clark, Edward T. *Designing and Implementing an Integrated Curriculum: A Student-Centered Approach*. Brandon, Vermont: Holistic Education Press, 1997.

Coalition for Self Learning. *Guidebook & Directory of Consultants for Creating Learning Communities.* Rangeley, Maine: Coalition for Self Learning, 2000.

Conrad, David. *Education for Transformation: Implications in Lewis Mumford's Ecohumanism.* Palm Springs, California: ETC Publications, 1976.

Dahl, Robert. Quoted in "The Strong Principle of Equality and the Archaic Origins of Greek Democracy" by Ian Morris. *DĒMOKRATIA: A Conversation on Democracies, Ancient and Modern.* Edited by Josiah Ober and Charles Hedrick. Princeton, New Jersey: Princeton University Press, 1996.

DeBruin, Jerry. *Wholistic Hands-On Science: An Interdisciplinary Guide to Science Concepts and Processes.* Parsippany, New Jersey: Good Apple, 1995.

Decker, Larry E. "The Leadership Legacy of Frank J. Manley." *The Evolution of the Community School Concept: The Leadership of Frank J. Manley.* Fairfax, Virginia: National Community Education Association, 1999.

---. "Frank Manley and Charles Stewart Mott: An Extraordinary Partnership." *The Evolution of the Community School Concept: The Leadership of Frank J. Manley.* Fairfax, Virginia: National Community Education Association, 1999.

---. "Epilogue: Looking Ahead." *The Evolution of the Community School Concept: The Leadership of Frank J. Manley.* Fairfax, Virginia: National Community Education Association, 1999.

Designs for Learning, Inc. "Community Learning Centers: Design Specifications." 1994. ERIC Document: ED 385 898.

Dewey, John. *The Ethics of Democracy.* 1888. Reprint, under the title "John Dewey—The Early Works, 1882-1898: 1882-1888, vol. 1," Carbondale, Illinois: Southern Illinois University Press, 1969.

---. *Democracy and Education.* Macmillan Company, 1916; New York, New York: The Free Press, 1997a.

---. *Experience and Education.* Kappa Delta Pi, 1938. Reprint, New York, New York: Touchstone, 1997b.

---. *OCTE (Outlines of a Critical Theory of Ethics.* 1891. Reprint, under the title "John Dewey—The Early Works, 1882-1898: 1889-1892, vol. 3," Carbondale, Illinois: Southern Illinois University Press, 1972.

---. *The Child and the Curriculum.* 1902. Reprint with a new introduction by Philip W. Jackson, Chicago: The University of Chicago, 1990.

---. *The School and Society.* 1900, 1915 (revised edition), 1943. Reprint, with a new introduction by Philip W. Jackson, Chicago: The University of Chicago Press, 1990.

Dewey, John and James H. Tufts. *Ethics.* New York, New York.: Henry Holt and Company, 1908.

Dryden, Gordon. *First Fundamentals.* United Kingdom: Accelerated Learning Systems Ltd., 1995.

Dryden. Gordon and Colin Rose. *Fundamentals Guidebook.* United Kingdom: Accelerated Learning Systems Ltd., 1995.

Edwards, Pat. "Frank Manley and the Community School Vision." *The Evolution of the Community School Concept: The Leadership of Frank J. Manley.* Fairfax, Virginia: National Community Education Association, 1999.

Eicholz, Hans L. *Harmonizing Sentiments: The Declaration of Independence and the Jeffersonian Idea of Self-Government.* New York, New York: Peter Lang, 2001.

Ezell, Bill. *Face the Flag.* Performed by John Wayne. DeVere Music Corporation (ASCAP), Batjac Music Company (ASCAP), 1973.

Flake, Carol L. *Holistic Education: Principles, Perspectives and Practices: A Book of Readings Based on "Education 2000: A Holistic Perspective."* Brandon, Vermont: Holistic Education Press, 1993

Fried, Robert L. "Toward Learning in Community." Ph.D. diss., Harvard University, 1976. Printed by *University Microfilms International*.

---. *Learning in Community: An Empowerment Approach.* Concord, New Hampshire: Office of Community Education, New Hampshire Department of Education, 1980.

Gardner, Francis. Quoted in "Political and Economic Liberalism in England" by Joyce Appleby. *Liberalism and Republicanism in the Historical Imagination.* Cambridge: Harvard University Press, 1992.

Gardner, Howard. *Frames of Mind: The Theory of Multiple Intelligences, Tenth Anniversary Edition.* 1983. Reprint, with a new introduction by Howard Gardner, New York, New York: Basic Books, 1993a.

---. *Multiple Intelligences: The Theory in Practice.* New York, New York: Basic Books, 1993b.

---. *The Disciplined Mind: What All Students Should Understand.* New York, New York: Simon & Shuster, 1999a.

---. *Intelligence Reframed: Multiple Intelligences for the 21ˢᵗ Century*. New York, New York: Basic Books, 1999b.

Gates, William H. <u>National Press Club Luncheon Press Club Series Website</u>. "Speech on the Estate Tax."
<http://www.npr.org/programs/npc/010511.wgates.html>
© 4 May 2001 <http://www.npr.org/ramfiles/exrad/010511.wgates.ram>.
4 May 2001.

Hansen, Mogens Herman. "The Ancient Athenian and the Modern Liberal View of Liberty as a Democratic Ideal." *DĒMOKRATIA: A Conversation on Democracies, Ancient and Modern*. Edited by Josiah Ober and Charles Hedrick. Princeton, New Jersey: Princeton University Press, 1996.

Hewitt, John P. *Self and Society: A Symbolic Interactionist Social Psychology, Seventh Edition*. Needham Heights, Massachusetts: Allyn & Bacon, 1997.

Hobbes, Thomas. *De Cive (On the Citizen: Cambridge Texts in the History of Political Thought)*. Translated and edited by Richard Tuck and Michael Silverthorne. Cambridge: Cambridge University Press, 1998.

Holden, B.   Quoted in "The Ancient Athenian and the Modern Liberal View of Liberty as a Democratic Ideal" by Mogens Herman Hansen.   *DĒMOKRATIA: A Conversation on Democracies, Ancient and Modern.*   Edited by Josiah Ober and Charles Hedrick.   Princeton, New Jersey: Princeton University Press, 1996.

Illich, Ivan.   *Deschooling Society.*   New York, New York: Harper & Row Publishers, 1970.

International Community Learning Center Network Website.   "The Whitepaper." 03 January 2002.   03 January 2002.   <http://www2.kanazawa-it.ac.jp/englishd/reber/clc1.htm >.

Jackson, Philip W.   Forward to *Dewey's Laboratory School: Lessons for Today*, by Laurel N. Tanner.   New York, New York: Teachers College Press, 1997.

Jeffs, Tony.   *Henry Morris: Village Colleges, Community Education and the Ideal Order.*   Nottinghamshire, England: Educational Heretics Press, 1998.

Jefferson, Thomas.   A Bill for the More General Diffusion of Knowledge, 1779.   In *Jefferson: Political Writings (Cambridge Texts in the History of Political Thought)*, edited by Joyce Appleby and Terence Ball, IV.2: 235-243.   Cambridge: Cambridge University Press, 1999.

---.   A Declaration by the Representatives of the United States of America, in General Congress Assembled [Jefferson's draft].   In *Jefferson: Political Writings (Cambridge Texts in the History of Political Thought)*, edited by Joyce Appleby and Terence Ball, II.5: 96-102.   Cambridge: Cambridge University Press, 1999.

---.   The Declaration of Independence [as amended and adopted in Congress], July 4, 1776.   In *Jefferson: Political Writings (Cambridge Texts in the History of Political Thought)*, edited by Joyce Appleby and Terence Ball, II.6: 102-105. Cambridge: Cambridge University Press, 1999.

---.   First Inaugural Address, 4 March 1801.   In *Jefferson: Political Writings (Cambridge Texts in the History of Political Thought)*, edited by Joyce Appleby and Terence Ball, III.9: 172-176.   Cambridge: Cambridge University Press, 1999.

---.   Letter to Dr. Benjamin Rush, 16 January 1811.   In *Jefferson: Political Writings (Cambridge Texts in the History of Political Thought)*, edited by Joyce Appleby and Terence Ball, VIII.11: 425-430.   Cambridge: Cambridge University Press, 1999.

---.   Letter to George Wythe, 13 August 1786.   In *Jefferson: Political Writings (Cambridge Texts in the History of Political Thought)*, edited by Joyce Appleby and Terence Ball, IV.5: 249-252.   Cambridge: Cambridge University Press, 1999.

---. Letter to James Adams, 28 October 1813. In *Jefferson: Political Writings (Cambridge Texts in the History of Political Thought)*, edited by Joyce Appleby and Terence Ball, III.16: 185-191. Cambridge: Cambridge University Press, 1999.

---. Letter to Joseph C. Cabell, 2 February 1816. In *Jefferson: Political Writings (Cambridge Texts in the History of Political Thought)*, edited by Joyce Appleby and Terence Ball, III.21: 202-206. Cambridge: Cambridge University Press, 1999.

---. Letter to Roger C. Weightman, 24 June 1826. In *Jefferson: Political Writings (Cambridge Texts in the History of Political Thought)*, edited by Joyce Appleby and Terence Ball, II.17: 148-149. Cambridge: Cambridge University Press, 1999.

---. Letter to Samual Kercheval, 12 July 1816. In *Jefferson: Political Writings (Cambridge Texts in the History of Political Thought)*, edited by Joyce Appleby and Terence Ball, III.23: 210-217. Cambridge: Cambridge University Press, 1999.

---. Letter to Thomas Law, 13 June 1814. In *Jefferson: Political Writings (Cambridge Texts in the History of Political Thought)*, edited by Joyce Appleby and Terence Ball, IV.19: 285-280. Cambridge: Cambridge University Press, 1999.

---. Letter to William Charles Jarvis, 28 September 1820. In *Jefferson: Political Writings (Cambridge Texts in the History of Political Thought)*, edited by Joyce Appleby and Terence Ball, VI.13: 381-382. Cambridge: Cambridge University Press, 1999.

---. Notes on Virginia: Query XIII. In *Jefferson: Political Writings (Cambridge Texts in the History of Political Thought)*, edited by Joyce Appleby and Terence Ball, IV: 326-327. Cambridge: Cambridge University Press, 1999.

---. Notes on Virginia: Query XIV. In *Jefferson: Political Writings (Cambridge Texts in the History of Political Thought)*, edited by Joyce Appleby and Terence Ball, IV.7: 256-260. Cambridge: Cambridge University Press, 1999.

---. Opinion on Residence Bill, 15 July 1790. In *Jefferson: Political Writings (Cambridge Texts in the History of Political Thought)*, edited by Joyce Appleby and Terence Ball, III.4: 159. Cambridge: Cambridge University Press, 1999.

---. Second Inaugural Address, 4 March 1805. In *Jefferson: Political Writings (Cambridge Texts in the History of Political Thought)*, edited by Joyce Appleby and Terence Ball, X.9: 530-535. Cambridge: Cambridge University Press, 1999.

Jensen, Eric. *Introduction to Brain-Compatible Learning*. San Diego, California: The Brain Store, 1998a.

---. *Teaching with the Brain in Mind.* Alexandria, Virginia: Association for Supervision and Curriculum Development, 1998b.

---. *Brain-Based Learning.* San Diego, California: The Brain Store, 2000.

Jewish Community Centers of Chicago Website. Jewish Community Centers of Chicago Organization. "About JCC." © 2000. 02 March 2001. <http://www.jccofchicago.org/about.html>.

---. "Adults." © 2000. 02 March 2001. <http://www.jccofchicago.org/adults/body.html>.

---. "Camp Chi." © 2000. 02 March 2001. <http://www.jccofchicago.org/chi/body.html>.

---. "Children." © 2000. 02 March 2001. <http://www.jccofchicago.org/children/body.html>.

---. "JCC Early Childhood." © 2000. 02 March 2001. <http://www.jccofchicago.org/infants/body.html>.

---. "JCC Early Childhood Programs." © 2000. 02 March 2001. <http://www.jccofchicago.org/infants/classroom.html>.

---. "JCC Early Childhood Programs." © 2000. 02 March 2001.
<http://www.jccofchicago.org/infants/kinder.html>.

---. "Home." © 2000. 02 March 2001.
<http://www.jccofchicago.org/body.html>.

---. "Totally for Teens." © 2000. 02 March 2001.
<http://www.jccofchicago.org/teens/body.html>.

Kelly, Kevin. *New Rules for the New Economy: 10 Radical Strategies for a Connected Word.* New York, New York: Penguin Books, 1998.

Knowles, Malcolm. *Self-directed Learning: A Guide for Learners and Teachers.* Englewood, New Jersey: Prentice Hall Regents, 1975.

---. "Creating Lifelong Learning Communities: Conceptualizing All Systems as Systems of Learning Resources." A working paper prepared for the UNESCO Institute for Education, Hamburg, Germany, January 1983.

Koehler, Jerry W. and Joseph M. Pankowski. *Transformational Leadership in Government.* DelrayBeach, Florida: St. Lucie Press, 1997.

Kofman, Fred and Peter M. Senge. "Communities of Commitment: The Heart of Learning Organizations." *Learning Organizations: Developing Cultures for Tomorrow's Workplace.* Edited by Sarita Chawla and John Renesch. Portland, Oregon: Productivity Press, 1995.

Laslett, Peter. Introduction to *Two Treatises of Government (Cambridge Texts in the History of Political Thought),* edited with an introduction and notes by Peter Laslett. Cambridge: Cambridge University, Press, 1988.

LearnLink Global Communication and Learning Systems Website. USAID LearnLink Project. 29 October 1999. 19 February 2000. <http://www.aed.org/learnlink/details.htm>.

Locke, John. *Two Treatises of Government (Cambridge Texts in the History of Political Thought).* Edited with an Introduction and Notes by Peter Laslett. Cambridge: Cambridge University, Press, 1988.

Luksik, Peg and Pamela Hobbs Hoffecker. *Outcome-based Education: The State's Assault on Our Children's Values.* Lafayette, Louisiana: Huntington House Publishers, 1995.

MacIntyre, Alasdair. *After Virtue, second edition.* Notre Dame, Indiana: University of Notre Dame, 1984.

Maier, Henry W. *Three Theories of Child Development: The Contributions of Erik H. Erikson, Jean Piaget, and Robert R. Sears, and Their Applications, Revised Edition.* New York, New York: Harper & Row, 1969.

Manley, Frank J., Bernard W. Reed, and Robert K. Burns. *The Community School in Action.* Chicago: Education-Industry Service, 1960.

Markley, O.W. and W. Harman. Quoted in *Designing Social Systems in a Changing World* by Bela Banathy. New York, New York: Plenum Press, 1996.

Maslow, Abraham H. *Motivation and Personality.* Third Edition, revised by Robert Frager, James Fadiman, Cynthia McReynolds, and Ruth Cox. New York, New York: Addison-Wesley Educational Publishers Inc., 1987.

Mayhew, Katherine Camp and Anna Camp Edwards. *The Dewey School.* 1936. Reprint, with an editor's forward, New York, New York: Atherton Press, 1966.

Mead, George Herbert. *Works of George Herbert Mead, Volume 1: Mind, Self, & Society from the Standpoint of a Social Behaviorist.* 1934. Reprint, edited and with an introduction by Charles M. Morris, Chicago: University of Chicago Press, 1962.

---. *Works of George Herbert Mead, Volume 3: The Philosophy of the Act.* 1938. Reprint, edited and with an introduction by Charles M. Morris, Chicago: University of Chicago Press, 1972.

Melby, Ernest O. "Frank Manley: A Giant in American Education." *The Evolution of the Community School Concept: The Leadership of Frank J. Manley.* Fairfax, Virginia: National Community Education Association, 1999.

Miller, Ron. *What Are Schools For? Holistic Education in American Culture.* Brandon, Vermont: Holistic Education Press, 1992.

--- et al. *Educational Freedom for a Democratic Society: A Critique of National Goals, Standards, and Curriculum.* Brandon, Vermont: Resource Center for Redesigning Education, 1995.

Moffett, James. *The Universal Schoolhouse: Spiritual Awakening Through Education.* San Francisco, California: Jossey-Bass Publishers, 1994.

Morris, Henry. The Village College: Being a Memorandum on the Provision of Educational and Social Facilities for the Countryside, with Special Reference to Cambridgeshire, 1924. In *The Henry Morris Collection*, edited by Harry Reé, 11-33. Cambridge, England: Cambridge University Press, 1984.

---.   Institutionalism and Freedom in Education, March 1926.   In *The Henry Morris Collection*, edited by Harry Reé, 34-43.   Cambridge, England: Cambridge University Press, 1984.

---.   Rural Civilisation, September 13, 1936.   In *The Henry Morris Collection*, edited by Harry Reé, 47-54.   Cambridge, England: Cambridge University Press, 1984.

---.   Post-War Policy in Education, July 31, 1941.   In *The Henry Morris Collection*, edited by Harry Reé, 55-74.   Cambridge, England: Cambridge University Press, 1984.

---.   Community Centres, January 1945.   In *The Henry Morris Collection*, edited by Harry Reé, 97-101.   Cambridge, England: Cambridge University Press, 1984.

---.   Liberty and the Individual, November 13, 1946.   In *The Henry Morris Collection*, edited by Harry Reé, 109-113.   Cambridge, England: Cambridge University Press, 1984.

---.   Architecture, Humanism and the Local Community, May 15, 1956.   In *The Henry Morris Collection*, edited by Harry Reé, 124-134.   Cambridge, England: Cambridge University Press, 1984.

Morris, Ian.   "The Strong Principle of Equality and the Archaic Origins of Greek

　　　Democracy."*DĒMOKRATIA: A Conversation on Democracies, Ancient and*

　　　Modern.   Edited by Josiah Ober and Charles Hedrick.   Princeton, New Jersey:

　　　Princeton University Press, 1996.

National Community Education Association, U. S. Department of Education, Policy

　　　Studies Associates, Inc., and American Bar Association—Division of Public

　　　Education.   "Keeping Schools Open as Community Learning Centers: Extending

　　　Learning in a Safe, Drug-Free Environment Before and After School."   1997.

　　　ERIC Document: ED 409 659.

---.   USAID LearnLink Project.   29 October 1999.   19 February 2000.

　　　<http://www.aed.org/learnlink/task/CLCs.html>.

National Education Association.   *Student Portfolios*.   West Haven, CT: NEA

　　　Professional Library, 1993.

Norton, David L.   *Personal Destinies: A Philosophy of Ethical Individualism*.

　　　Princeton, New Jersey: Princeton University Press, 1976.

---.   Afterword: A Philosophical Appraisal to *Education for Creative Living: Ideas and*

　　　Proposals of Tsunesaburo Makiguchi, edited by Dayle M. Bethel and translated by

　　　Alfred Birnbaum.   Ames, Iowa: Iowa State University Press, 1989.

---. *Democracy and Moral Development.* Berkeley: University of California Press, 1991.

O' Rourke, P.J. *Why I am a Conservative.* Hollywood: Center for the Study of Popular Culture, Rolling Stone Magazine, not dated.

Ostwald, Martin. "Shares and Rights: 'Citizenship' Greek Style and American Style." *DĒMOKRATIA: A Conversation on Democracies, Ancient and Modern.* Edited by Josiah Ober and Charles Hedrick. Princeton, New Jersey: Princeton University Press, 1996.

Palmer, Parker. *Let Your Life Speak: Listening for the Voice of Vocation.* San Francisco, California: Jossey-Bass, Inc., Publishers, 2000.

Parson, Steve R. "Afterschool Programs: A Beginning, Not an End!" Working paper, Virginia Polytechnic Institute, August 2000.

---. *Transforming Schools into Community Learning Centers.* Larchmont, New York: Eye on Education, 1999.

Pendell, Richard C. "Excerpts from the *Community Education Journal,* November 1972 In Memoriam." *The Evolution of the Community School Concept: The Leadership of Frank J. Manley.* Fairfax, Virginia: National Community Education Association, 1999.

---. "Frank Manley Remembers: The Last Interview." *The Evolution of the Community School Concept: The Leadership of Frank J. Manley.* Fairfax, Virginia: National Community Education Association, 1999.

Plato. "The Republic." *Great Dialogues of Plato.* Translated by W.H.D. Rouse and edited by Eric H. Warmington and Philip G. Rouse. New York, New York: Penguin Books, 1984.

Procunier, Douglas. "The Origin and Evolution of the Community School in Flint, Michigan: The Frank Manley Influence." *The Evolution of the Community School Concept: The Leadership of Frank J. Manley.* Fairfax, Virginia: National Community Education Association, 1999.

Reber, Michael. "Community Learning Centers: A Eudaimonistic Model for Education." Working Paper presented to The East-West Center, Honolulu Hawaii, Thursday, March 18, 1999a.

---. "Community Learning Centers and Sustainability: Reengineering Education for the 21st Century." In *Pathways to Sustainability: The Age of Transformation*, edited by Andrew Cohill and Joseph Kruth, chapter 8. Lake Tahoe, Nevada: Tahoe Center for a Sustainable Future, Arete, Inc., 1999b. <http://ceres.ca.gov/tcsf/pathways/chapter8.html>.

Reigeluth, Charles. "A Third-Wave Educational System." In *Systems Design of Education: A Journey to Create the Future.* Englewood Cliffs, New Jersey: Educational Technology Publications, Inc., 1991.

Smith, Adam. *The Wealth of Nations.* Edited and with an Introduction, Notes, Marginal Summary, and Index by Edwin Cannan, with a new Preface by George J. Stigler. Chicago: The University of Chicago Press, 1976.

Smyre, Rick. "Building Capacities for Transformation." *Guidebook & Directory of Consultants for Creating Learning Communities.* Rangeley, Maine: Coalition for Self Learning, 2000.

---. "Leadership in Transformation." Working Paper. Center, Communities of The Future. Gastonia, North Carolina, 14 March 2001.

---. *Developing Knowledge Democracy Capacities for the 21st Century.* Working Paper. Center, Communities of The Future. Gastonia, North Carolina, 1999.

Suzuki, Motoshi. "The International University: A 25-Year Experiment in Restructuring University Education." In *Creating Learning Communities: Models, Resources, and New Ways of Thinking about Teaching and Learning.* Edited by Ron Miller. Brandon, Vermont: The Foundation for Educational Renewal, 2000.

Tanner, Laurel N. *Dewey's Laboratory School: Lessons for Today.* New York, New York: Teachers College Press, 1997.

Taylor, Charles. *Sources of the Self.* Cambridge, Massachusetts: Harvard University Press, 1989.

---*The Ethics of Authenticity.* Cambridge, Massachusetts: Harvard University Press, 1991.

Tishman, Shari, David N. Perkins, and Eileen Jay. *The Thinking Classroom: Learning and Teaching in a Culture of Thinking.* Needham Heights, Massachusetts: Allyn and Bacon, 1995.

Tocqueville, Alexis de. *De La Démocratie en Amérique (Democracy in America).* Translated, edited, and with an introduction by Harvey C. Mansfield and Delba Winthrop. Chicago: The University of Chicago Press, 2000.

Tuck, Richard and Michael Silverthorne. Introduction to *De Cive (On the Citizen: Cambridge Texts in the History of Political Thought)*, by Thomas Hobbes. Cambridge: Cambridge University Press, 1998.

University Corporation for Atmospheric Research (UCAR) Website. "Windows to the Universe." 1995. 24 April 2001. <http://www.windows.ucar.edu>.

USAID LearnLink Project. *Benin Country Paper.* USAID Academy for Educational
Development (AED). Summer 1999.

U.S. Department of Education Website. H. R. 6: "Improving America's Schools Act of
1994," 103rd Congress, 2nd session, January 25th, 1994. 24 January 2001.
26 February 2001. <http://www.ed.gov/legislation/ESEA>.

---. H. R. 6: "Improving America's Schools Act of 1994," 103rd Congress, 2nd session.
24 January 2001. 26 February 2001.
<http://www.ed.gov/legislation/ESEA/sec10902.html>.

---. H. R. 6: "Improving America's Schools Act of 1994," 103rd Congress, 2nd session.
24 January 2001. 26 February 2001.
<http://www.ed.gov/legislation/ESEA/sec10905.html>.

---. H. R. 6: "Improving America's Schools Act of 1994," 103rd Congress, 2nd session.
24 January 2001. 26 February 2001.
<http://www.ed.gov/legislation/ESEA/sec10907.html>.

---. H. R. 1804: "Goals 2000: Educate America Act," 103rd Congress, 2nd session,
January 25th, 1994. 24 January 2001. 26 February 2001.
<http://www.ed.gov/legislation/GOALS2000/TheAct/>.

Bibliography

U. S. House of Representatives: Office of the Law Revision Counsel Website.

      Title 20.   26 February 2001.   <http://uscode.house.gov/title_20.htm>.

Vermont Constitution, Chapter I, Article 7.

---.   Chapter II, Section 68.

Wallach, John R.   "Two Democracies and Virtue."   *Athenian Political Thought and*

      the Reconstruction of American Democracy.   Edited by J. Peter Euben, John

      Wallach, and Josiah Ober. Ithaca, New York: Cornell University Press, 1996.

Werner, Heinz.   *Comparative Psychology of Mental Development.*   New York, New

      York: Science Editions, Inc., 1948.

Westbrook, Robert B.   *John Dewey and American Democracy.*   New York, New

      York: Cornell University Press, 1991.

Whitehead, Alfred North.   *The Aims of Education and Other Essays.*   New York, New

      York: The Free Press, 1929; New York, New York: The Free Press, 1967.

Yarbrough, Jean M.   *American Virtues: Thomas Jefferson and the Character of a Free*

      People.   Lawrence, Kansas: University Press of Kansas, 1998.

www.ingramcontent.com/pod-product-compliance
Lightning Source LLC
Chambersburg PA
CBHW062101050326
40690CB00016B/3164